WJEC
CBAC

Teacher's Book

GCSE English/English Literature

Roger Lane

Consultants
Barry Childs
Ken Elliott
Margaret Graham
Stuart Sage
Ted Snell
Ken Welsh

OXFORD
UNIVERSITY PRESS

Great Clarendon Street, Oxford OX2 6DP

Oxford University Press is a department of the University of Oxford.
It furthers the University's objective of excellence in research,
scholarship, and education by publishing worldwide in

Oxford New York
Auckland Cape Town Dar es Salaam Hong Kong Karachi Kuala Lumpur
Madrid Melbourne Mexico City Nairobi New Delhi Shanghai Taipei Toronto

With offices in

Argentina Austria Brazil Chile Czech Republic France Greece Guatemala
Hungary Italy Japan Poland Portugal Singapore South Korea Switzerland
Thailand Turkey Ukraine Vietnam

Oxford is a registered trade mark of Oxford University Press
in the UK and in certain other countries

British Library Cataloguing in Publication Data

Data available

ISBN- 13: 978 0 19 831496 7

ISBN- 10: 0 19 831496 5

10 9 8 7 5

Designed and typeset by Mike Brain Graphic Design Limited

Printed in Great Britain at Basingstoke Press

Author's acknowledgements

Thanks to Ysgol Penweddig, Aberystwyth, Ceredigion; Dyffryn Taf,
Whitland, Camarthenshire and Bedwas High School, Caerphilly for
providing sample responses in large numbers, and to Elizabeth Evans for
organizing them.

Contents

Introduction

This book for teachers is largely built upon sample answers written by students to questions and tasks that are to be found in the pages of the *Students' Book*. These are intended to inform both teachers and students about the set standards in GCSE English and English Literature. Each response is assessed according to the grade criteria for GCSE, which are printed near the start of each section of the book. The *Students' Book* contains a wide range of texts and individual tasks which are essentially for the classroom, not the examination hall, and they have obviously not been subject to scrutiny by the WJEC paper setting committee. Many of the questions in the *Students' Book* are accompanied by detailed support material, thus qualifying to some degree the achievement of students in the responses.

Increasingly throughout the GCSE years, the study of sample answers has been regarded as an essential for teachers and students. It is not expected, though, that the pages of this book will be remorselessly pursued in detail – rather that teachers will select judiciously and use several different approaches. For example:

1 Teachers might simply use sample answers as quick-check standardizing material 'behind the scenes' when assessing their students' responses.

2 Teachers might choose to photocopy sample answers without the comments and estimated grades, setting students the task in small groups to assess the responses in some detail.

3 Sample answers with the comments could be given to students in small groups with the instruction that they discuss the 'split grade' awarded and come to their own decision.

4 Students might be asked to annotate and/or proof-read sample answers (especially less successful ones) to focus their attention on consolidation through the grades.

5 A few written/printed answers from the class (anonymously) could be added to the samples and groups asked to provide a rank order of achievement.

6 In the spirit of providing variety and keeping up their students' morale, teachers are advised to tackle some of this evaluation work on sample answers without requiring students to write their own answers.

There is a world of difference between, on the one hand, distributing a set of past or specimen papers for students to work through at their own pace in class and, on the other hand, concentrating on one targeted question for a focused lesson. The *Students' Book* and the *Teacher's Book* are constructed on the principle of selecting and highlighting part-sections of WJEC papers in order to teach skills and organize lessons to best effect.

Section 1: Prose reading

Introduction

Section A of English Paper 1 tests the skills of reading by asking a series of questions on a piece of literary prose. These skills are covered in the first section of the *Students' Book* within four units:

1.1 Personal response
1.2 Deeper meaning
1.3 How does the writer...?
1.4 Empathy

These units focus on different types of question that are asked in the examination, concentrating on the key features of the questions while recognizing that, in practice, the question types overlap considerably. In the exam, a series of four (or sometimes five) questions will be asked, but these are by no means likely to be focused in sequence in the way of the four units above. The 'literary' text itself will always determine the questions worth asking, and students can be assured that personal response, inferential meaning and, not least, insights into the writer's use of language are always appreciated, provided there is a genuine attempt to answer the question set.

The texts in Section 1 of the *Students' Book* were selected in line with the regulatory authority (QCA/ACCAC) prescription for a major prose writer from the English literary heritage with a well-established critical reputation to be represented in the GCSE English specification. Most of the writers featured in Section 1 unambiguously fit that bill; others will have more disputed claims. However, it is the reading skills that count, and the combinations of texts and questions are surely challenging enough for all candidates.

The amount of support for the students varies within a unit. The first task is always given detailed support to re-state the importance of developing an answer fully. The final task in each unit is presented in a way that requires students to apply independently some of the advice given along the way. All tasks are recognizable as exam-style tasks, but the last one in each unit encourages students to be rigorous in terms of timing and organization. Grids are provided to help students structure some of their answers, but these can only help to some extent, so they appear occasionally, rather than for every task. It is vital that students learn to think for themselves.

Two or three responses are given for each of the tasks in this section. Comments on the responses are included at the end of each unit. The responses were written by GCSE students in roughly the 15 minutes that might be allocated to a single reading question in the exam. Teachers might wish to follow this principle when using the *Students' Book* – students read and discuss to 'a state of readiness', then answer the question 'against the clock'.

Mark scheme

This generalized mark scheme uses phrases that are widely used in WJEC examination marking. Teachers and students can work out in which of these broad bands an answer fits and where within the band it might belong.

Grades

u/G
Nothing attempted or struggles to engage with the question and/or the text.

F
- ♣ Understanding of the main events.
- ♣ Simple comments with occasional reference to the text.
- ♣ Unselective copying.
- ♣ Unsupported assertions.

E/D
- ♣ Simple comments based on surface features of the text.
- ♣ Awareness of more straightforward implicit meanings.
- ♣ Some reference to 'what happens'. Possibly some attempt to touch on the issue of 'how'.
- ♣ An understanding of the events and some sense of character and feelings.

C/B
- ♣ Appropriate material selected from the text to reach valid, sensible conclusions. Clear inferences based on textual evidence.
- ♣ Engagement with the issue of 'how', though possibly relying on some narrative or 'spotting' of key quotations.
- ♣ Some attempt to comment on narrative technique. Some grasp of writer's technique.
- ♣ Clear understanding of the events and a sense of the character's tone and attitude.

A/A*
- ♣ Appropriate detail from the text explored with depth and insight. Thorough as well as perceptive.
- ♣ Well-considered personal response based on appropriate evidence from the text. Text analysed and explored, showing insight into technique and use of language. Overview of the text.
- ♣ Selective account of events, showing insight into the character's attitudes and viewpoints. Thorough, perceptive, coherent, sounding like the character.

Unit 1.1 Personal response

Tickets, Please by D.H. Lawrence

♦ **What are your impressions of John Thomas from these lines?**

i

We get the impression that John Thomas is a bit of a lad who flirts with the women conductors on the trams. He uses girls for a good time and got the nickname Coddy because that's all he thinks about. I get the impression that he's vain because he thinks he can woo them. But on the other hand he doesn't care about the bad reputation he has got himself in half a dozen villages. He walks out on the women after he's done with them — but it notes that he's choosy and will only flirt with a conductor providing she's attractive. 'Malice' and 'scandal' are all adjectives that surround John Thomas and he's a cunning character because he takes advantage of the fact that all the men are fighting abroad. I think he's a bit of a coward because he's not fighting in the war, but he would probably argue that he's doing his part for the war effort.

ii

I get the impression that John Thomas loves himself but there are no really malicious thoughts in his actions. I believe from reading the piece that the words 'malice', 'fury' and 'scandal' are a bit harsh. I just believe that he's having fun, even though what he is doing is wrong. I get the impression that he's not well liked around because people call him 'coddy' purposefully, they know he doesn't like being called that. But the words 'malice' and 'scandal' are still too strong to describe his actions in my opinion. I just get the impression that he's out just to have some fun while he's still young. I get the impression that John Thomas thinks himself as a bit of a Romeo! That any girl will fall at his feet. I think he believes that he can get any girl he wants. He thinks of himself as a bit of a lad who can pick up and drop any girl when he chooses. The impression that I get of him is that he is a bit of 'pretty' boy because he doesn't go to the war, he just stays at home with the women while the other men are away. But at the end of the day the biggest impression that I get from reading the passage is that there is no malice in what he is doing. I don't believe that he is doing it to harm or hurt the girls. I just get the impression that he is just making the most and having fun with his life.

iii From the first few lines in this passage we get the impression that John Thomas is quite an aggressive man. It says in the passage, 'His face sets in fury,' this shows his anger in his personality. We see that he is blatantly not fond of his nickname and despises anyone who calls him this.

When said in the passage that there is a 'considerable scandal about John Thomas' you get the impression that he is a troublemaker and has caused a lot of upset with many people. The passage says, 'He flirts with the girl conductors'. This makes him sound confident and slightly full of himself. He takes the girls for granted and uses them, and then moves on to the next one. The line 'then he flirts with the newcomer: always providing she is sufficiently attractive.' This gives you an awful impression of him. When I read these lines, I was disgusted. He only chooses the attractive ones because they are the only ones good enough for him. He is very vain and selfish. He seems to always think of himself and doesn't take other people's feelings into account.

John Thomas seems to be a big flirt and he thinks very highly of himself. He also seems to be surrounded by women and he has not gone to fight in the war. This could be due to his feminine side and he is not enough of a man to go to war. He treats the women like this and keeps on doing it because the women are willing and not surrounded by men because they are at war.

Nineteen Eighty-Four by George Orwell

♣ **What are your thoughts and feelings about the opening of this story?**

i The story starts by giving details of the weather on some day in April. There is a description of a middle-aged man rushing into Victory Mansions in a bid to escape out of the windy cold weather outside. It also says that he couldn't get in fast enough without a swirl of gritty dust following him indoors. The first description we get of inside the building is that it smelt of boiled cabbage and old rag mats. It gives us the impression that it's a very old place. Another suggestion that it's a very old place is that the light is unreliable and the man knew it wouldn't be working during the day. It's something to do with the electric. The man had to walk up seven flights of stairs which was hard work for him with the ulcer on his ankle. He also describes a huge poster on the wall in his opinion

WJEC TEACHER'S BOOK

too big for indoors of a man and wherever the man went the eyes of the poster were watching him. This adds a spook to the mansion. It said 'Big brother is watching you' which again adds a spook too that somebody else is secretly watching your every move.

ii The opening of the story is very strange and gives me a feeling as though something may happen but the author is not giving anything away. The story begins all bright and positive but as soon as the man enters the block of flats the author changes to dull, bleak and almost negative imagery. This is as though the block of flats and the world outside are two different and contrasting worlds. Right from the beginning the author makes you think – 'the clocks were striking thirteen'. It could be a twenty-four hour clock yet there is something strange in the way he has worded it. The way the author has described the wind as 'vile' suggests that the block of flats is set in a bleak place or the author has some kind of dread towards the wind. 'The hallway smelt of boiled cabbage and old rag mats' uses the senses to describe exactly what the block of flats were like. It is also a smell that would be strange to your nostrils and would make you feel ill. 'An enormous face, more than a metre wide' is a line which you'd think is ominous as the way the author has described it – it is not normal to have a face so large. The line 'electric current was cut off during daylight hours' seems strange to me as this is not normal practice in a block of flats. I also didn't understand how cutting the electric during the daylight hours was preparation for 'Hate Week'. It all seems odd to me. The words 'varicose ulcer' seemed ominous to me as a man of thirty-nine from my knowledge would not yet have varicose veins.

EVIDENCE FROM THE TEXT	IDEA	EXPANDED COMMENT
'the clocks were striking thirteen'	Strange	*This is unusual. It could just be a 24-hour clock, but it makes us think right from the start.*
'in an effort to escape the vile wind'	Bleak	
'a swirl of gritty dust'		
'smelt of boiled cabbage and old rag mats'		*It probably turns your stomach and is likely to be a dreadfully sickly and stale smell.*
'an enormous face, more than a metre wide'	Ominous	
'the electric current was cut off during daylight hours'		
'Hate Week'		
'a varicose ulcer'		
'one of those pictures which are so contrived that the eyes follow you about'		
'BIG BROTHER IS WATCHING YOU'		

Consider the Lilies by Iain Crichton Smith

♣ **What are your first thoughts and feelings about the meeting between the old woman and Patrick Sellar?**

i

My first thought is that the two characters are completely different. The old woman is very polite and kind, for example, offering him a cup of tea even though that would mean she would have to go to a lot of trouble to do so. The meeting seems awkward, Patrick Sellar kept hitting his whip against the bench and the old lady waited a while for him to speak. The description of the man is quite frightening, he doesn't seem friendly at all. He has an unwelcoming look to him, I think the old woman is a bit put off by this. But she doesn't show it, because she is polite and he is a guest in her home. The man grunts in response to her question. This again suggests that he is rude and has been brought up without having manners. She feels uncomfortable in her own home and she shouldn't.

When Patrick talks he doesn't seem to make much of an effort to have a flowing conversation. He talks boldly and to the point. When he tells her in the end that she has to leave her home, he doesn't break the news to her gently. He doesn't seem to feel sorry for her either.

ii

My first impressions of the old lady are how well mannered and courteous she is towards visitors, 'Wouldn't be polite to keep a stranger outside'. However the man/visitor is very different. He has been portrayed as having no manners or social skills, 'surprised that he didn't tell her to sit down'. They are two very different people with different social skills. The man is rather blunt and has no emotion. 'All I have to say to you can be said here.' He's only there to do his job and then he shall leave. He has no time to be polite or friendly.

The old woman must have felt intimidated by him and his presence, 'He kept hitting his whip against the bench and even though this irritated her she didn't ask him to stop.' The man did not want to sit down. This emphasises that he will not be staying, he'll be gone as soon as he's delivered the bad news. He's a very ill mannered man. The man 'grunted' when the lady asked him a question. This was no way to answer an old lady. He has no respect for her. The old lady thinks that he's there about the pension. She had no idea and had not been warned. The news was to come as a shock to her.

The man dominates the old lady 'I'll tell you what I came for.' He's in control of the conversation. He has no manners, 'she wondered why he didn't say thank you' then realised that perhaps he's not that kind of well-mannered man.

iii My first thoughts about the old lady were of how well mannered and courteous she was. It was obviously a strain for her to have to stand to greet the man, but she managed to do so.

The old lady was surprised that he didn't tell her to sit down, as if he did so it would express his good manners in being courteous in return to the old lady. The old lady greeted the man with 'good day' and expected him to return the friendly comment, but the only reaction she received from him was a grunt. The old lady didn't believe it to be polite to leave a stranger outside the door, so instead of staying on the doorstep to speak to him, she walked in leading the way for the man to follow.

The man didn't sit on his own accord and only sat on the bench after the lady signalled for him to take a seat. Although the man hitting his whip against the bench was irritating she didn't mention it to him, as this would have been rude and ill mannered. The old lady guessed incorrectly what the reason for the man visiting was. She thought it was because of the pension, but it wasn't.

The old lady offered the man a cup of tea, although it would mean a lot of work for her. But she was prepared to do it. The man answered without even saying thank you, which of course was rather shocking to the old lady, because she was so well mannered.

Oranges Are Not The Only Fruit by Jeanette Winterson

♠ **What are your impressions of the young girl in this passage?**

STUDENTS' RESPONSES TO THE QUESTION

i In this extract we read about a girl called Jeanette. From the extract, it seems like she has very low self-esteem and seems to think that her school friends don't like her because of her religious background.

In this extract, it also sounds like Jeanette is feeling sorry for herself about the dinner monitoring. When she is describing it, she describes it in a very negative way. She describes all the bad things and doesn't say if there is anything good about it. She lists all the bad bits of dinner monitoring and she describes the children in her school and what they say to her and call her. She also says about the teacher helping her with her work and her Auntie Betty thinking she was going to die. She lists everything that is wrong with her school life and doesn't think about the things she is thankful for. She feels sorry for herself and needs and wants sympathy.

Also, at the end of the passage I get the impression that she respects her mother when she says that her mother heals the sick. It sounds like she looks up to her mother and envies her.

ii

Although Jeanette is quite self-conscious and lonely, she tries her hardest and is very proud, 'I was anxious to do well.' She realises that it's hard to fit into a category, 'I couldn't seem to learn anything or win anything.' You get the impression that she doesn't fit in properly. 'I knew they thought I couldn't read or anything.'

Her mother plays an important role in her life. She looks up to her mother and when the teacher asked her if her mother was a nurse she replied, 'No, she just heals the sick'. Jeanette doesn't seem to have any confidence. Her class shouted at her for smelling like gravy! Jeanette admits that she doesn't fit in, 'I'd done my very best to fit in!' Jeanette seems to be grown up for her age. This can be seen when asked by her teacher to write an essay on holidays, instead of writing the same old thing about fishing or Disneyland, she chose to write about 'Colwyn Bay with our church camp'. She is open and from this we can see the contrast from her and her fellow pupils. You get the impression that she is innocent. Her class and her are worlds apart.

iii

The girl is someone who is very unlucky according to her, 'I couldn't learn anything or win anything.' She had also been drawn to be dinner monitor three times. The girl then goes on to explain what a dinner monitor does. There seems to be nothing good about it and during the description I began to feel sorry for her, especially when she got shouted at for smelling of gravy, as that didn't seem to be her fault. You get the impression that the girl is very depressed, from 'sometimes I tried to clean it off, but today I was too unhappy.' We then go on to learn about the girl's very religious background, having to spend six weeks in church camp. She doesn't seem to think religion is helping her, 'I'd be even less able to cope with any of it.' The girl tries her hardest in her work and tries very hard to fit in with the rest of the children. The girl finds it difficult to fit in mainly because her life's so different. The other children wrote about gardens and frogspawn, but the girl wrote about her church camp and her mum being a healer. I thought the girl was brave, hard working and trying her hardest to fit in in a new school and I felt sorry for her as she seemed to be very unlucky.

Unit 1.1 Comments on the student responses

Tickets, Please by D.H. Lawrence

There is some fairly detailed support given in the *Students' Book* for this question, but credit to the three students responding here for taking advantage and setting a good standard. All three answers select material well and make valid and sensible comments. Answer (i) is direct, lacking a bit of care and caution in the way it asserts that John Thomas is 'a bit of a coward'. The most obvious limitation though is the attempt to deal with 'malice' and 'scandal', both named incorrectly as adjectives, and neither understood at all. This was an unnecessary diversion in a 'personal response' setting. (Grade: D/E.) Answer (ii) pursues a line of defence for John Thomas quite effectively and, in so doing, shows reasonable understanding of some of the key vocabulary (Grade: B/A.) Answer (iii) takes a different, though perfectly valid, approach, one that criticises John Thomas, pulling no punches in saying, 'I was disgusted'. (Grade: C/B.) You may not agree that answer (ii) is the most independently thoughtful of the three answers – but all three did quite well exploring a compact piece of text with an unfamiliar setting.

Nineteen Eighty-Four by George Orwell

The first answer here offers a clear, though superficial, description before generalizing reasonably well that the building in the extract was old. Only at the end of the answer, however, does this student pick up on the prompts of *strange*, *bleak* and *threatening* with the tentative use of 'spook'. Perhaps this passage would prove to be difficult in an exam for many students because of its 'mystery' qualities. (Grade: D/E.) Answer (ii) is much more successful – it engages at length and in detail with the oddities of the scene. This student is confident enough to be able to deal wisely with the uncertainties that an unseen passage can present. (Grade: B/A.)

Consider the Lilies by Iain Crichton Smith

All three of these answers are full of sensible comments. However, answer (i) has some uncertainty or imprecision in 'doesn't seem friendly', 'has an unwelcoming look'. (Grade: D/C.) Answer (ii) moves forward more swiftly and purposefully, with insights into the relationship between the visitor and the old woman – 'intimidating', 'dominates' and 'in control'. (Grade: B/A.) Answer (iii) is possibly more dependent on tracking of the narrative (no bad thing!), rather than summarizing the relationship, but the commentary is sound and deceptively skilful. There is a lot of weighing-up in answer (iii), and this nearly puts it on a par with the second answer. (Grade: C/B.) The three answers imply that it is easier for students to deal with the attitude of the woman in this question than the man, who tends to be seen as plain rude, rather than uneasy and nervous.

Oranges Are Not The Only Fruit by Jeanette Winterson

None of the three answers for this extract acknowledges the prompt in the *Students' Book* that there is humour in the writing, but they all recognize in different ways that the girl is out of the ordinary. Answer (i) perhaps tries too hard to make the evidence fit the initial point about self-esteem, but finds it difficult to make points of interest about dinner-monitoring and Auntie Betty. It is fair to say that answer (i) is a little unconvincing. (Grade: D/C.) Answer (ii), however, makes some useful points about the girl's reaction to her situation and how she tries hard to fit in at the school. The points are made rather tentatively for much of the answer, but comments that 'she is rather grown up' and also that she is 'open' and 'innocent' are good, despite the apparent contradiction. The last sentence offers a useful summary too. (Grade: C/B.) Answer (iii) also makes some sensible inferences backed up with evidence, perhaps getting nearest to the heart of the passage with a consistent view of the girl being stoical in the face of misfortune. (Grade: C/B.) Answers (ii) and (iii) are both fairly successful responses, reminding us that 'personal response' does allow for differing viewpoints, provided there is some justification.

Unit 1.2 Deeper meaning

Tickets, Please by D.H. Lawrence

♠ What is Annie's attitude to her relationship with John Thomas?

i Annie firstly really likes John Thomas. She does not think that the relationship will last, but she likes him anyway. She has a spare boyfriend in case things do not work out with John, so this makes me think that she does not trust him very much, or else she would be faithful to John Thomas. Annie doesn't like men very much or else she would treat John better by being faithful and not use the other one either. Annie does not want John to be a nocturnal presence, this means she is tired of him visiting her in the night and she wants to go out with him in the day too. She wants people to see her with John so she can show off. By the end of the passage, Annie has broken up with John and she is devastated. She wishes they were still together and feels empty without him. But it serves her right for seeing someone behind his back.

ii At first, Annie's attitude towards the relationship with John Thomas is pessimistic and doubtful. She does not want to risk a relationship with him, 'Annie walked out with John Thomas, though she kept her own boy dangling in the distance'. This quote basically says that she was keeping someone else as insurance just in case the relationship between her and John Thomas didn't work out. As time goes on, Annie's attitude towards John Thomas changes 'Annie liked John a great deal'. John is now something special to her. Calling John Thomas a nocturnal presence shows that he was very shy and not talkative. The fact that Annie didn't want him to be a nocturnal presence shows that she is very enthusiastic about the relationship. After their separation, Annie had many different attitudes at many different stages. First off she was surprised, 'startled'. Secondly she goes through a series of emotions including 'fury, indignation, desolation and misery.'

iii In the text you find out a lot about Annie's attitude to her relationship with John Thomas. In a way she is very cautious, but she is also opportunistic. The text starts with a sentence that gives the reader some indication of Annie's attitude towards John, 'So Annie walked out with John Thomas, though she kept her own boy dangling in the distance,' which shows us that Annie is unsure of her relationship with John and keeps another boy 'dangling', waiting just in case things don't work out. 'Annie liked John a good deal,' which suggests something a bit special about this relationship and that although she is unsure she still likes him a lot. There is a lot in the third paragraph that suggests the type of relationship that Annie and John have. 'Annie wanted to consider him a person, a man,' this shows that Annie doesn't seem to know John that well but would like to get to know him better. She wanted more out of the relationship than just 'a nocturnal presence', she wanted companionship and conversation as well as a physical relationship. We also find out that they both want different things from the relationship, 'she started to take an intelligent interest in him,' but 'he hated intelligent interest'. In other words, she wanted commitment and he didn't. Annie then states that John 'aroused the possessive female in her,' which is the reason the text gives for him leaving her. Annie's feelings towards the relationship come out in the way she reacts when he leaves, 'she was not surprised'. This suggests that she knew the relationship wasn't working and it came as no surprise. Her true feelings are revealed, 'she wept with fury, indignation, desolation and misery.' She was sad but also angry about the end of the relationship.

TEXTUAL REFERENCE	EXPLANATION/COMMENT
... walked out with John Thomas, though she kept her own boy dangling in the distance.	*She's hedging her bets, keeping the other lad as a reserve! This might suggest some doubts about John Thomas.*
... liked John Thomas a great deal.	*'A great deal' suggests something a little special.*
... wanted to consider him a person, a man ...	
... did not want a mere nocturnal presence ...	
... she prided herself that he could not leave her.	
... the possessive female was aroused in Annie.	
... startled, thrown out of her count.	
... she had been so very sure of holding him.	
... she wept with fury, indignation, desolation, and misery.	
... she determined to have her own back.	

ATTITUDE?	EXPANSION
Casual or committed?	*She is committed, not at all casual, despite keeping her 'own boy' in tow. She seems to be looking for a full-time relationship.*
Easy-going or serious?	
Positive?	
Proud?	
Emotional?	

Young Adolf by Beryl Bainbridge

♣ **How do Adolf and Alois behave in this passage? Refer closely to the text in your answer.**

i

Adolf is very lazy, he sits around the house doing nothing, just eating and sleeping. He is not ill and is just generally being lazy. Alois comes home from work, he seems very fed up with Adolf's laziness. He shouts at the sleeping boy, he is very angry and tells Adolf to pack his bags. Adolf is frightened by this I think. He doesn't know where to go. The author shows Alois is very angry by the adjectives he uses like 'fumed'. Alois is very angry with Adolf for being disrespectful in his home. He throws a metal art piece across the room, narrowly missing Adolf. Alois after the climax in the story seems very shaken up. He is very upset that he lost his temper to such a degree. He tells Bridget that he could have killed Adolf. We find out that it is years of anger that has built up. He doesn't know what to do, he feels that him and Adolf have grown so far apart.

ii

From the passage we see two different people behaving completely differently. Adolf is very lazy. He doesn't do any work around the house and just lets Alois and his wife do the work for him. We learn a lot from the passage about Adolf's behaviour before Alois confronts him. All Adolf does all day is sleep and eat. When Alois comes home from work and confronts Adolf he doesn't react that differently. We don't see massive amounts of emotion from Adolf. He just stays very quiet. This is shock. The only emotion we see from Adolf is shock. He doesn't know what to do or say. Alois must have really surprised him and perhaps Adolf had never seen Alois react like this before.

Alois reacts completely differently to Adolf. Alois is very angry and he is in the dominant position when it comes down to what happens in the living arrangements. We see Alois behaving like a mad man and from what we see in the other room, behaving out of character. When he confronts Adolf he goes mental and nearly kills him. But when he realises what he nearly did he completely changes and in a way is worried that he could behave like that.

iii Firstly Alois is angry throughout this passage although tries not to be. He loses his temper, 'I'm not angry,' he shouted. Alois even had 'little purple veins in his cheeks'. This shows how angry he feels. Logically Alois does not want to be angry but he can't help his raw emotion. We see this at the end of the passage, ' "God forgive me," whispered Alois.' Here Alois shows instant regret for his anger. Another example of Alois clinging to his patience is, 'I've no objection to a man lounging about til Kingdom Come...' Here Alois' strength of feeling is shown in the way that he uses exaggeration, 'Kingdom Come'. Words like 'roughly', 'fumed' and 'shouted' are used to describe Alois' actions and in doing so convey his anger. In a stark contrast, once he has thrown the item at Adolf and is regretting his actions, the words used are 'whispered', 'forlorn' and 'prowled'. These in contrast show now that Alois is much more subdued and controlled, as opposed to the previously explosive nature of his behaviour.

Adolf is seemingly unaware of Alois' feelings until he is awoken. It seems as though Adolf had no idea of the anger and ill feeling towards him. We see this element of feeling bewildered in the repetition, ' "Go," said Adolf. "Go where?" ' The author uses a simile with schoolboy imagery, 'like a penitent schoolboy', giving ideas of naiveté and youth and suggesting that he was nothing more than a naughty little boy. We see the idea of Adolf being weak and bewildered, 'He crouched there clasping and unclasping his hands' and 'his face had lost its look of stupor and acquired a haunted expression.' Here Adolf's feelings of desperation are conveyed in his actions, or lack of actions.

On the Black Hill by Bruce Chatwin

♠ **How do the Colonel and the Major try to encourage local men to join the Army?**

i

(i) *The colonel and the major persuade the men by using a number of emotional appeals and tactics. They built up an atmosphere by showing the audience film pictures of the brave men seen fighting for the king, 'Tommies', and this makes the men in the audience feel inspired and also the women to tell the men to go and fight. The men want to impress the ladies. He includes the audience frequently by referring to them as 'YOU' — to say that it is their responsibility. He builds up the atmosphere by describing the 'two classes of person in this country' and the audience felt patriotic. The colonel is quick to backtrack and turn his mistake of forgetting Wales to his advantage by telling the Welsh to go with the major to Brecon. He was clever and used persuasive language in an effective way. 'England expects of every man: namely to do his duty.'*

ii

The first point that struck me was the pictures of the Tommies shooting on the film slide. These pictures troubled the men and got them frustrated. The pictures also made them eager to see more or even made them anxious to move there. When the major stood up and announced that 'They are your enemy' this makes their blood boil. In that sentence there is a dramatic pause. This emphasises what's coming up next. The major announces that so they know who but then leaves them hanging on for a second to know what they've done. I believe that the major also shows the men how much he thinks of the Germans by saying 'that' instead of 'they'. This encourages the men by knowing that they are dirt or smaller than them.

Colonel Bickerton gives the men the emotional 'feel sorry for me' speech. He makes the men feel guilty and in the wrong so they feel duty to join the forces. I believe that the writer has used the woman in the blue hat to give us a message about 'YOU' going to war. It's very unusual to see a woman telling her son that he should join and her sentence sounds very fake.

iii Firstly the major wins the respect and admiration of the crowd by showing 'stirring' slides of British soldiers overseas. He furthers this by showing them a slide of Kaiser Wilhelm II of Germany, 'your enemy'. He has excited and interested the crowd and stirred hatred towards the opposition.

The Colonel then starts by also earning their respect from the crowd by speaking of his own son at war and what the country's plight meant to him. He was making a statement that implied that he was no better than the crowd, that he and his family were not exempt from war. He then goes on to shame 'shirkers' as he called them, by declaring that fighting is a duty young men had, 'to their king, their country ... and their womenfolk'. The way he referred to a duty to defend womenfolk was a direct appeal to young men's masculinity. The major also speaks of aristocracy and their duty to the country. He glamorises war, gives it an air of honour, dignity and makes the men feel obligated to fight.

The two have obviously managed to gain the attention of the crowd, 'Again, the hand rose with fluid grace and, again the crowd fell silent.' Along with the shouts of agreement from the crowd, this makes the fact that the volunteers 'rushed forward to press their names on the major', seem inevitable.

He makes the campaign not only appeal to the individual ' ... says he needs you, he means YOU,' but also to all types and groups, again in his reference to aristocracy and to the Welsh. 'For in my veins Welsh blood and English blood course in equal quantities'. In this part the words he uses also make you feel honoured and obligated to fight, such as 'loyal', 'beloved' and 'most gallant'.

The Woman in Black by Susan Hill

♣ **How do the narrator's thoughts and feelings change during this extract?**

i

The narrator's thoughts were to continue on to the next village when a strange feeling invades him and he stops. He was thinking of his next meal when he has the urge to stop. The narrator feels that he has to look eastwards, when he sees the marshes and thinks how beautiful and how it draws him in. He feels attracted to the marshes and feels that his whole being is drawn to it. The narrator realises how his spirit is changing while looking at the marshes. He thinks about if his friends and family will notice the change that he has so obviously seen in himself.

ii

At the beginning of the passage, the narrator is cheerful and is very monotonous in the way he describes his bike ride. The narrator seems to have planned his journey. The narrator also comes across as organised and not having excitement in his life, but usually he sees fields and farms. In the middle there is a sudden change, from predictable to the opposite — unpredictable. The narrator seems to look at everything differently. It's as though someone has changed and influenced him and it's drawing him in. He has curiosity and wants to find out more. At the end of the second paragraph the narrator is drawn in and his feelings towards life change. In the last paragraph it is as though he has analysed his life and is thinking what he has missed in life. He realises he has new sensations and he reacts and behaves differently. He realises the change in himself only in a day, it's as though he is connected on a spiritual basis.

iii The narrator's thoughts and feelings change quite dramatically during the extract. At the beginning he thinks about his 'simple' day and what he'll be doing such as enjoying some 'bread and cheese and beer for lunch'. It's another ordinary day and he's just cycling and enjoying the view. His days are quite monotonous and I think at the beginning he's just doing the same thing – he says 'another' country inn which tells us that he's possibly been to one earlier or the previous day. However his 'normal' day changes when he comes across the extraordinary house. His thoughts are concentrated on the house and he cannot think of anything else. His actions become faster and he seems to think about more things. The punctuation reflects the change in pace. At the beginning the narrator uses one very long sentence to reflect the slowness and the way his day 'flows'. However, once he sees the house the punctuation changes. The sentences are much shorter and more commas are used, 'and there they lay, those glittering, beckoning, silver marshes.' At the beginning the author doesn't use many interesting adjectives, e.g. 'cold', 'bright'. This shows that it was another ordinary day, but after the sighting of the house he uses more lively and colourful adjectives, such as 'glittering'. This mirrors this exciting new encounter and emphasises how extraordinary it is. We also see 'and' used at the beginning instead of a comma, 'bread and cheese and beer'. This prolongs the sentence and makes it more boring. However, as his feelings change the author uses commas to make lists 'my step to be quicker, everything I saw was brighter, it's outlines more sharply ...' He also repeats the word 'my' – 'my imaginings, my longings, my curiosity, my whole spirit'. This indicates that he feels he's losing himself and his identity under 'some sort of spell'. It also tells us that he's scared of losing his identity and is trying to fight the spell to save himself and his ordinary life.

Unit 1.2 Comments on the student responses

Tickets, Please by D.H. Lawrence

The first answer is a purposeful response to the question about Annie's attitude, but all of the comments are in a simple light, lacking the subtleties that a close reading of the text would offer. The language employed in this answer, including 'faithful' and 'devastated' suggests the student is not seeing the uncertainty and confusion in Annie. (Grade: D/C.)

Answer (ii) understands something of Annie's contradictory thoughts but cannot explain them satisfactorily. In some cases, such as 'nocturnal presence', this answer reveals a potential misunderstanding. The student has, however, been prepared to struggle and take a risk to strive for deeper meaning. (Grade: C/B.)

Answer (iii) is altogether more comfortable with the complexity of the relationship, and leads with the double-edged nature of Annie's attitude to it. There are shrewd comments both on 'nocturnal presence' and 'possessive female' and how the relationship is seen differently by Annie and John Thomas. (Grade: B/A.)

Young Adolf by Beryl Bainbridge

Answer (i) tracks the events of the passage quite well, but does not comment particularly well on them. The comment that Adolf is 'frightened' by Alois's rage is not incorrect, but it is rather a weak response to a key paragraph on Adolf's behaviour. The commentary continues in simple vein, mainly with comments about Alois, accurate, but inconclusive. (Grade: E/D.)

Answer (ii) is perhaps not significantly different from the first answer, but it appears to have a better balance between the coverage of each of the individuals. It also has more ambitious ideas: 'dominant position', 'behaving out of character', 'confronts'. Adolf''s behaviour is usefully described as being the result of 'shock'. (Grade: D/C.)

Answer (iii) has lots of quotations, but it is not these alone that make the answer a strong one. It is the student's willingness to explore the details of the text that is pleasing. The answer captures the drama well and thrives on the mixed emotions and tension. (Grade: B/A.)

On the Black Hill by Bruce Chatwin

Answer (i) makes some good, clear points, but some of them are rather general. (Grade: D/C.) There is a greater sense of tracking the text in detail at the start of answer (ii), but this is not really maintained. There is, though, rather more of a thoughtful attempt at explanation. (Grade: C/B.)

Answer (iii) is much more confident and consistent than the previous two, and matches details with an understanding of the ways the Colonel and the Major encourage their audience. (Grade: B/A.) In fact, the Colonel and the Major use persuasive techniques in a way that is more commonly seen in transactional non-fiction and media texts.

The Woman in Black by Susan Hill

Answer (i) comfortably recognizes the change in the thoughts and feelings of the narrator, but remains uncertain about putting words to the change, apart from an attraction to the beauty of the marshes. (Grade: E/D.)

Very clearly, the second answer offers more – from the contented routine (rather clumsily identified as 'monotonous') to the contrasting spiritual experience. However, in answer (ii) the landscape is not cited as responsible for the change, which the student seems to convey as coming from within, rather than as a result of external influences. (Grade: D/C.)

Answer (iii) is obviously longer and, though not offering consistent quality, does set up contrasts between pub lunches and 'the 'exciting new encounter'. The answer is one that engages with the nature of the change and attempts to explain it, though curiously reference to 'mysterious silence' and 'haunting, strange beauty' is avoided. Some of this response is not well-focused: witness the seemingly ubiquitous reference to adjectives and a fairly strained mention of 'and' replacing a comma. (Grade: C/B.) This is a question requiring concentration on changing thoughts and feelings, rather than techniques of writing.

Tickets, Please by D.H. Lawrence

♠ **How does the writer successfully create the effect of being on a tram journey?**

STUDENTS' RESPONSES TO THE QUESTION

i Most of the passage is a description of everywhere and everything that is passed on the tram journey. This gives the picture of what it would look like if you were travelling along in a tram looking out of the window. It describes the view as they leave the town as going 'off into the black industrial countryside'. There are a lot of adjectives to describe this, such as 'ugly', 'little', 'grimy', etc. It gives a very detailed description in a small passage. Also there is quite a lot of description on the tram's movement. It describes the tram going up the hill, down dale, tilting away in a rush past cinemas and shops, reckless swoops downhill, bouncing the loops. It is a very descriptive passage with many adjectives in it. This creates a dull atmosphere of the area, quite poor and grey. It is done well by the writer's choice of words and phrases, such as 'grimy cold little market places' and 'long ugly villages of workmen's houses'.

ii The story opens with a set-piece commentary of the tram journey. These lines are full of descriptions and much detail and the scene is one of movement and action. The writer describes the tram's journey — describing all that it passes, we get the feeling that it covers a lot of ground quickly because there are a lot of commas in the passage and also a lot of descriptions of many different scenes. The writer notes that the tram goes up/downhill and we get the feeling that we are on a rollercoaster. The places he describes are industrial villages and towns — very ugly and gloomy in his view.

The fact that there are very long sentences gives the rollercoaster effect and the rich vocabulary gives a sense of excitement and danger. The sentences are breathless and this gives the feeling that the tram stops and starts. Adjectives such as 'swoops downhill' makes the twists, turns, the slow climbs and the racing sensations even more dramatic. There's a sense of relief when the tram comes to a halt.

The adjectives used to describe the surroundings are dark and barren. The personification of the tram add to the mood and atmosphere.

iii This is a piece full of movement and excitement. The writer conveys the tram's journey in one sentence. It is a long and rhythmic sentence that almost rolls off the tongue to reflect the rhythmical, long and steady journey of the tram. In the middle the tram is static, this is also reflected in the piece by the shorter sentences and punctuation. As the train restarts its journey home again the writer again uses one long, constant sentence to convey the movement.

There is a lot of very effective descriptive language in the piece to create a very real image for the reader. There are several effective modifiers, such as 'slithering', 'stark', 'bulky' and 'black'. The images created are all very dark and bleak. This may give us an insight into what the writer feels about industry. This piece is full of life, 'a rush', 'plunges' and 'somewhat dare-devil' are but a few examples of the excitement. The excitement however is solely that of the tram, the surroundings are portrayed as bleak and there is no mention of passengers. Despite this the writer gives the surroundings some element of personification or animal features, such as 'fat gas-works' and 'breathless slithering'.

Another way the writer gives the reader the impression of fast travel is through his use of 'we', bringing the reader into the tram's journey.

Decline and Fall by Evelyn Waugh

♦ **How does the writer make this passage humorous and amusing?**

STUDENTS' RESPONSES TO THE QUESTION

i The author makes this passage humorous and amusing by setting it in the early twentieth century. The characters have posh speech which is funny in some people's eyes. The author has given the characters funny names such as Lady Circumference, Pennyfeather and Mr Prendergast. These names prevent the reader from taking the characters seriously.

The storyline is amusing as it is based on a race that has disastrous events preventing the race from happening. When Tangent got shot no one seemed shocked about it. This was also amusing because they gave him some cake and got on with the race. They didn't seem to care that much. Basically, the writer makes this passage humorous with funny names, funny happenings and funny characters. Even the last line is amusing, '"On your marks! Get set!" Bang went the pistol, this time without disaster.'

ii *The writer uses a number of techniques to add humour to the passage. The first thing you notice are the humorous names used for the characters like Lord and Lady Circumference. They make you view the characters as being silly and less serious before you even get to know them. This immediately adds humour to the text. Lady Circumference's comments throughout the text add humour. 'Shockin' noise' lets you get to know the character better and her snobbiness during the start adds to the humour of the chaotic race by letting you see the snobby character causing a disaster and not being able to control things. She is a rude character even though she's supposed to be a 'lady'. She insults Tangent, 'the boy can't run an inch' and corrects 'loudly' what clump of trees the course went round: ' "goes round the clump of elms ..." "Beeches," corrected Lady Circumference'.*

This I suppose is humorous because Paul is made a fool of in front of everyone. The incident with the gun is very funny. You can picture exactly what's happening. The use of exclamation marks adds surprise and feelings. You have the apology from Mr Prendergast almost before you realise what is happening.

iii *The writer makes the passage humorous and amusing by giving strange names to the characters to begin with, 'Lady Circumference'. Here the writer uses a mathematical term that introduces the character and keeps the image of the character humorous and not so serious. I believe also that there is a pun here as 'circumference' means the length of the perimeter of a circle. It is trying to tell us that she is a 'round' woman. Also the things that Lady Circumference says create amusement, 'Shockin''. This is not proper educated tongue and the fact that she doesn't appreciate what the band is doing suggests that she is a fraud and behaves as though she is in a higher class than she really is.*

Another way the writer creates humour is the imagery. 'She sat down with the doctor next to her and Lord Circumference on the other side of him'. The image the reader gets is very amusing, picturing one man between two huge people. Also there follows the quote, ' "Pennyfeather," cried the doctor above the band. "Start them racing" '. This quote shows that the doctor wishes to finish the day as soon as possible and also the fact that he has to 'cry' above the band tells us that things are very chaotic or that the people either side of him are causing problems with his voice!

AREAS OF HUMOUR	COMMENT/EXPLANATION
Mathematical names – Circumference etc	*Silly, but quite funny. Prevents the reader from taking them too seriously . . .*
The words and behaviour and attitude of Lady Circumference. Several examples.	*Rude in an upper-class sort of way, even to her own family. Larger-than-life character.*
The shooting – and the reactions to it.	
Prendergast – drunk.	
Tangent – stuffing himself with cake.	

Billy Liar by Keith Waterhouse

♣ **How does the writer convey a sense of frustration in Billy Fisher as he tells his story?**

i

In this piece we see how the author uses a dinnertime conversation in the first person, from Billy's point of view to convey his feelings. His frustrations become more obvious in the second half of the piece, 'I took a deep breath and made it obvious I was taking a deep breath.' Here he is trying to convey his frustrations. His actions are described in detail 'heavy sigh' and 'clenched teeth'. Towards the end of the piece we have the moronic and patronising pepper pot and salt cellar demonstration.

ii

In these lines Billy is trying to tell his family about his ambition, his dream in life, and they do not seem to have a clue what he is talking about. The mother is patronising by saying things like he is not capable of getting a decent job. His gran seems to take no notice or interest whatsoever.

Billy feels angry and frustrated in this extract and this anger is expressed by using 'flaming' and breaking things down so that his parents can understand.

The writer uses repetition, 'they knew', to cause an effect of frustration and uses capital letters, 'B-double-O-N'. He describes Billy's 'heavy sighs' and 'deep breath' to emphasise his impatience and frustration. The writer also uses sarcasm to try and show his impatience once again, 'this line — together with a rhubarb-rhubarb chorus'. The writer also uses words like 'hysterical calm' to create an effect of frustration.

iii In the extract, the writer creates a dramatic situation around the breakfast table, with Billy up against his mother, father and gran, telling them of his plans to write a comedy for Danny Boon. There is a lot of lively dialogue in this passage, with each of the characters making their own comments. No matter how hard Billy tries, or how obvious he makes the situation, they still don't fully comprehend what he's telling them. He resorts to using the pepper pot and the salt cellar to represent his material and Danny Boon. The writer creates a sense of frustration, because we, the readers, know exactly what Billy is trying to say, therefore there is a sense of tension created by the chasm between what is and what isn't understood.

The author tells us what will happen in a colourful way at the very beginning of the extract, with the image of the old no 14 tram and the festering arguments which adds to the frustration. We know from the start that he won't be understood. This sense again of knowing that something will happen adds to the tension, even though it is also quite funny.

Billy's thoughts tell us that they knew beforehand about everything that is being spoken about here, but still they plead ignorance. When someone knows something but you still have to tell them about it, it is frustrating and this happens in the extract. His parents and gran add to his suppressed anger by questioning him and throwing in absurd comments like 'Why does he always leave the white of his egg?' These non-constructive comments do nothing to help the situation. The picture vividly creates a chaotic atmosphere of tension and frustration, ending with yet another negative comment for Billy from his father. We've seen the whole event through Billy's eyes, with the other members of the family portrayed as ignorant and ridiculous.

HOW THE WRITER CONVEYS A SENSE OF FRUSTRATION IN BILLY

What happens in these lines:	*Textual references and comments:*
How Billy thinks and feels:	*Textual references and comments:*
How Billy's father, mother and grandmother behave:	*Textual references and comments:*
The writer's technique and use of language:	*Textual references and comments:*

The Voyage by Katherine Mansfield

♣ How effectively does the writer create the sadness of the parting?

i

In the first lines the writer tells us of how 'father sounded stern but looked tired and sad'. It shows us that although Fenella's father was trying to be strong and hide his emotions, his true feelings were being shown. It also shows how young children notice people's emotions far easier than older people.

The writer has used dialogue to create the atmosphere. We learn that they are leaving and Fenella's father isn't going. 'God bless you' is used also by the father and her grandmother. This gives a sense of religiousness and sadness.

The writer uses very descriptive language describing the grandmother's hand, her glove and how it was worn through on her ring finger. How the grandmother sobs, 'God bless you, my own brave son' creates the thought of pride and sympathy. She wants god to bless him, her son.

When he says goodbye to Fenella, the writer uses simple adjectives like cold and wet to describe his moustache. Cold and wet are unhappy, depressing words, they aren't very comforting.

ii

The writer creates a sad mood in many ways. At the beginning he uses the word 'cry' to describe the voice on the loud speaker. This is very effective because it tells us that Fenella is very upset and therefore hears the voice as a cry. The extract is also very rushed and mirrors the feelings of panic of the characters and that the time they have is very brief and very precious. The short sentences also portray the anxiousness of grandma and Fenella and emphasises that there isn't enough time for a proper goodbye, 'He wouldn't look at her'. The writer also describes things that the characters wouldn't normally do, 'To her surprise Fenella saw her father take off his hat'. This indicates that her father feels it's his last chance to see them and is trying to tell his mother how much he loves her. This also emphasises the sadness of the situation and how uncertain they feel.

iii This passage is about a girl and her grandmother leaving on a boat and saying goodbye to the girl's father. There is use of dialogue in the passage which shows us how each character is acting and how they are feeling. In the first paragraph Fenella sees that her father looks tired and sad.

In the second paragraph the grandmother talks in short sentences, 'Go now. You'll be left. Go now, Frank. Go now.' This shows us that the grandmother is in a hurry to leave which could mean that she can't bear the thought of leaving her son anymore.

In the third and fourth paragraphs we get to know how much the grandmother and her son care for each other when the father 'clasps Grandma in his arms' and says, 'God bless you, Mother.' To this the grandmother answers with, 'God bless you, my own Brave son.' This shows us that the grandmother and son don't want to leave each other.

There is a good use of adjectives in the passage which creates an image of the scene, 'black threaded gloves', 'cold wet moustache'. Fenella is also very sad and nearly crying in the fifth paragraph. She asks her father anxiously, 'How long am I going to stay?' which is a sign that she'd rather stay with her father and doesn't want to go.

The last paragraph is the most upsetting in my opinion because it's a scene between the father and his young daughter. She is obviously upset as she cries, 'Father' and thinks 'she must be going away forever'. The last sentence is effective. It is about the dark wharf slipping, sliding edging away from them which could also mean that the family are being separated and are slipping, sliding away from each other.

Unit 1.3 Comments on the student responses

Tickets, Please by D.H. Lawrence

Answer (i) begins with two creditable, but quite general statements. The details that follow are tentative, with the selection of adjectives offering little to suggest an appreciation of the effect of the writing. The movement of the tram is eventually described, but without any sense of excitement. Given the richness of the passage, this first answer cannot be said to grasp the writer's technique with any confidence. (Grade: E/D.) Answer (ii) tries harder to engage with the journey and makes something of the rollercoaster effect and notes both 'excitement and danger'. It is still mostly rather general and it ends disappointingly, but has some moments of promise along the way. (Grade: D/C.) Answer (iii) very clearly exceeds the other two in quality, with a conviction from the start as to the qualities of the passage. There is plenty of well-selected detail and also moments of insight. The student succeeds in bringing the journey to life again. (Grade: B/A.)

Decline and Fall by Evelyn Waugh

Answer (i) opens with a sentence that cannot really be credited, even though we might just be able to see what the student means by linking it with the next sentence! Most of the rest of the answer does earn credit, though entirely on the level of spotting and describing. (Grade: E/D.) Answer (ii) attempts to comment with 'silly', 'chaotic', 'snobby', 'rude character ...'. Despite some clumsiness, there is clear evidence of an engaging, probing approach, though there is certainly more scope for explicit comments on the writer's technique(s). (Grade: C/B.) However, the student who wrote the final answer may be guilty of trying too hard – the points about perimeters and 'shockin' are forced and rather superfluous to the main case. The comments continue to be rather laboured and, though they are not without merit, they lack the easy insight of answer (ii). (Grade: D/C.) It is worth stating that humour is not easy for students to analyse.

Billy Liar by Keith Waterhouse

Answer (i) is not particularly long. It opens with a comment that tries with limited success to make something of the significance of Billy as narrator. It also hints at the build-up of frustration, but quotes and explains awkwardly. Two further quotations are offered, plus a final, detached comment on Billy's behaviour. In all, it is a response of unfulfilled potential. (Grade: D/C.) Answer (ii) has some good, individual comments and some apt selection of detail. (Grade: C/B.) The third answer is very clearly the strongest here, even though, unlike the other answers, it does not make use of the most obvious features of Billy's frustration. However, the opening sentence establishes a focus on the question and an overview of the passage. It is a particular strength of the answer to show a sustained understanding of the relationship between the dialogue of the mother, father and gran and the narrative of Billy. There are key details covered as well, but it is the quality of the overview that particularly impresses here. (Grade: B/A.)

The Voyage by Katherine Mansfield

Each of these three answers has merits. Answer (i) is quite sensitive and makes valid points throughout, though the student seems to have difficulty linking the points cohesively. The answer touches on, but does not develop a critical point about the young girl's view of the whole experience. The comment at the end on 'unhappy, depressing words' confirms the limitations of the answer. (Grade: D/C.) Answer (ii) has good instincts for the emotional impact and significance of the parting, but in terms of writer's technique the statement 'The extract is also very rushed' is something of a *faux pas*. (Grade: C/B.) Answer (iii) is both sensitive and also a little analytical, offering several comments about techniques (dialogue, the little girl's perspective, the grandmother's speech patterns, descriptive qualities). Again, a more confident student might have made these points more explicitly. (Grade: B/A.)

Unit 1.4 Empathy

Tickets, Please by D.H. Lawrence

♠ **Imagine you are Annie. Write down your thoughts and feelings about what has happened on this particular night.**

i

I can't believe what I have done. Well, what we all did! It wasn't just me but I felt so angry. How could he do that to all of us?

After we attacked him I couldn't bear looking at him knowing that I actually liked him too.

And making him choose was wrong but he did choose me. That made me feel as if I had won but I had to say something, 'I wouldn't touch him'. Maybe it was wrong, but the girls might have turned on me as well. But saying I didn't want him wasn't true.

ii

I … I think I like him. The way he stared at me that night — his eyes were full of anger, hatred. But still he chose me. I didn't want to say what I did. It was so hard to say but I had to. I couldn't show that I liked him still. I feel so … it was my fault that we tortured him but he deserved it. He's been a cheating pig and he needed to learn his lesson. That night I felt in power over him for a change. I feel tortured for torturing him. I wonder if the other girls feel the same. I hope they do then I wouldn't feel so bad. When he chose me I felt triumphant because he'd chosen me over everyone else. But I don't know if I want to be chosen. I hate him but I love him. I can't make up my mind. I don't know if the girls suspected anything. Why did I ask him to choose? If I hadn't I would never feel this way.

The way he walked off, face closed, his head dropped. I felt so guilty. They did wait for him to look at them so maybe they all felt the same as I did — all wanting him to look and choose them. I don't know how I feel. I had to make him choose. I had to know which one of us he really wanted. But the way he said my name, his voice was full of malice.

Tickets, Please by D.H. Lawrence

POINTS OF RELEVANCE IN THE PASSAGE	WHAT ANNIE MIGHT SAY DIRECTLY
Coddy's hostile eyes looking at her.	*He stared at me, hating me…*
'Speak!' 'You've got to choose!' 'Choose your girl, Coddy.'	*I had to make him choose, I had to know which one of us he really wanted.*
Puts her face 'devilishly' near his. 'And you'll get your neck broken if you play any more tricks, my boy.'	*I felt in control, I felt as if there was an evil strength running through me.*
John Thomas chooses Annie; the girls' reaction.	*He chose me and for a moment I felt triumphant because … but …*
Annie's reaction: 'I don't want him …' etc.	
The silence, followed by John Thomas putting himself back together. The girls' reaction at this point.	
The ending. The dejected image of John Thomas. Last words from the girls, then Annie.	

The Ragged Trousered Philanthropists by Robert Tressell

♣ **Imagine you are Jack Linden. At home, you tell your wife about the events of the day at work.**

i

I could feel Misery standing there for minutes on end, but I decided to ignore him and just carried on smoothing down the surface before I started painting. The trouble is he doesn't want a proper job doing, he just wants it all finished double quick speed. And if I started doing that there will be no quality in my work at all, just quantity. You know how people say that quality is better than quantity. I think if I rush my job something one day is going to go wrong and he will give me the sack and I wouldn't like that very much, would I?

Do you know that today in work, Easton, who was working on a plank, was so upset that he was scarcely able to stand. With his brush in his hand he fell off and made a loud noise on the floor, poor him.

ii

Every worker is talented but we're all under appreciated and under paid. He was complaining that I'd spent too much time on the doors. He was shouting and preaching. The man's impossible! I tried to answer him back but I was trembling so much I couldn't say anything. I knew that he could take my food away. Our food. But I knew he couldn't hurt me so I decided to answer him back. I had to have a chance to defend myself. I explained that I had to clean the work down before I painted but he doesn't understand things like that. He shouted at me again and he made me feel so small that I could hardly hold the pumice stone because I was trembling so much. Misery was still shouting and I wondered who would be next. He started to walk around the house, looking for an excuse to shout some more. He made everyone so nervous that no one could do their job correctly. Poor Payne nailed his thumb and Bundy got a deep gash in his finger. He was even too scared to bind it while Misery was still there. Because of this, all the tiles were covered with blood. Easton, who was working on a plank, was so scared that his brush fell to the floor with a crash! That's the effect this man has on people.

iii Work was terrible today. That old windbag, Misery we call him, the manager! He's a whiny fool who prefers fast work compared to a good job. He showed up twice today, as if the first time wasn't bad enough. When he came down the second time today, I knew I was in for it, because he saw me working on the door this morning. I kept quiet and went about my usual business; when he approached my stomach was terrible. You know, that bad feeling? I honestly felt like I'd been punched in the guts. You know how bad that man makes me feel. I get worried every time he comes round. I'm afraid I'm going to get kicked to the kerb. I want to keep the bread on the table, but with that … that … that fool hanging around, how can I?

It's not just me that gets affected, it's all the lads. They feel the same way as I do. Today's society has no place for guys like me. There aren't any jobs, especially for guys my age. I hate to say it but I need Misery. I mean he's always yelling at us to speed things up. He reminds me of an Egyptian slavedriver cracking his whip over prune-like slaves working under the looming sun. But if he wants it done fast then how can we do it right? He's got to be reasonable. If the walls are a bit weak or the plaster isn't set out properly, he's going to go on and on about poor workmanship. Then he'll have our heads.

I'm glad you weren't there to see us dear. We were a real mess. Payne was laying new floorboards when Misery drew near, like the grim reaper. Payne slammed his finger under a hammer, didn't he? Wouldn't be surprised if it's broken. I don't even want to get started on Bundy. For now, I'll have to play by Misery's rules, because he holds all the cards. The future and health of my family depend on his conscience.

Cold Comfort Farm by Stella Gibbons

♣ **Imagine you are Flora Poste. You write immediately after these events to tell your best friend in London about your initial experience at Cold Comfort Farm.**

i

Dear Lorna,

How have you been lately? Hope you're well. I am writing to you by letter because email is so impersonal today. I went to visit Cold Comfort Farm last Saturday. I was dropped off by Adam Starkadder with a horse (Viper) pulling the cart. Viper was quite a vicious horse with a bad attitude. Anyway, I was at Cold Comfort Farm because I was meeting some cousins of mine I hadn't ever seen before in my life. As the horse and cart pulled up to the farm I feared we were going to slam right into the fence, but we somehow averted the danger.

We approached one of the nearer buildings and a blinding beam of light seemed to shine out and I heard Adam give out a cry. I immediately began to panic, but I eventually realised that his cry was joyful not fearful. I looked and saw that it was being anxiously opened by a gaunt cow's (at least that's what I think they call them) nose. I did not find this very promising and I wish to return to you as soon as possible.

Best wishes, Flora.

ii

Dear Julia,

Hello friend. Sorry I haven't contacted you sooner but I have been busy. I arrived on a dark night with no warmth around me. When I arrived at the station there was a carriage waiting for me. He was a kind man, directing me in every way. When we arrived the road had disappeared into a hedge. I decided to walk with Adam. He works on the farm and he was a driver and he was wearing old trousers with holes and a farmer jacket. But he was a good gentleman. As we were about to open the door we saw a nose of a gaunt cow. I thought to myself this was not promising. But in a matter of time a deep voice was heard. I panicked in case they thought I was a bit too overdressed. I turned and saw Judith. I thought to myself was my lipstick the wrong shade because she was not looking at me properly. As I was so tired I said I'm going to bed and I would see them all in the morning.

Write soon, Flora.

iii Dear Charlotte,

How are you? I'm fine I suppose. I've arrived safely at Cold Comfort Farm. It is rather remote and primitive here though compared with London. But nothing I can't deal with. My cousin Adam Starkadder picked me up from the station in his cart drawn by a Viper. The conversation on our journey was rather blunt as he insisted on calling me Robert Postes child. I am nearly twenty-one, hardly a child any more.

It is very different to London here. The event that's caused the most excitement so far was when a cow – Feckless – opened the cow shed door in greeting. My cousin was practically jumping for joy. My cousin's fashion sense is very unusual. She wore an unnecessarily red shawl and a tumbling mass of untidy hair hangs down her back. I suppose they don't know much in the way of fashion when they live in the middle of nowhere and it's probably more about practicality, but even I can be practical!

There was a rather odd silence when I put my hand out in greeting. At first I thought it was because my lipstick was the wrong shade or my blouse was lightly creased from the journey. I thought it was the same situation as when the Indian first fixed his gaze upon the great Columbus, and for the first time a Starkadder had fixed their eyes on a civilised being. Then again, this might not be the case. What do you think? I think I need to get to know them better first. I don't know how long I'll be staying with them. This place is a little gloomy, but it might look better by daylight I suppose.

Best wishes, Flora.

Extraordinary Little Cough by Dylan Thomas

♣ **Imagine you are Jean. The day after these events you write an entry in your diary. You include your thoughts and feelings about meeting the boys.**

i

I had a wonderful day. I met the most wonderful boy, but now I'm confused because I know that Dylan loves me. I'm not sure what to do. I'm definitely in love with Brazell. I was so excited when Brazell and I were in the tent. My head was on his shoulder. It was so romantic. I feel awful now. I know that Dylan likes me so much. Somewhere in my heart I do feel for Dylan but it's nothing like the feelings that I have for Brazell. I was so impressed with what George did, running on Rhossilli sand. I think I may have feelings for George. O Diary, what should I do? I'm so confused. I'm sure I have strong feelings for Brazell but I'm not sure about Dylan. Somebody help me, I need to sort it out. I shall have to talk to Dylan. I will tell him that I love someone else. I will tell him that I don't love him in the same way that I love Brazell.

ii

Walked up the cliff with Dylan by my side today. He seems to like me. I don't blame him really, who doesn't? He is a nice boy, but as we went on up the hill, I saw someone much better! I saw a really handsome boy sitting on the beach. Dylan told me his name is Brazell and that he is a bully. I'm sure he's trying to put me off him and is just being spiteful, because he wants me for himself. Brazell was very tall and had dirty trousers.

When we got to the tents, Dylan gave me an apple, but I wanted a cigarette! Who wants a pathetic little apple! I'm not a child anymore. At last — I sat next to Brazell inside the tent. We sat close together so that is a sign that he must like me. I nestled my head on his shoulder and he didn't seem to mind at all. I felt nervous and really excited about it. I really like him. Dylan kept looking over at us. I don't think he was very impressed. He was jealous, probably, and who can blame him?

iii Today I had a very exciting day. I met four boys! They were all out camping, so I decided to join them. The first boy I spoke to, Dylan, seemed quite interested in me.

He was very talkative until I asked about a very handsome boy called Brazell, who I had spotted earlier. As soon as I asked him who this boy was his tone of voice changed. It was as though he was jealous of the interest I had shown in Brazell. Dylan tried his hardest to put me off Brazell. He told me how he never combed his hair and was a bully. I thought of this as a matter of opinion, as what I had seen of Brazell was lovely and nothing Dylan said was going to put me off.

Later on in the night I met Brazell and instantly grew even fonder of him. I sat by Brazell in the tent and rested my head on his shoulder. He was perfect.

I felt as though we were being watched. It was a really weird feeling. Later on I realised that it was Dylan. It was as though he was obsessed. He'd offered me an apple earlier in the day, like some kind of teacher's pet! But I didn't want it; I really wanted a cigarette instead!

Unit 1.4 Comments on the student responses

Tickets, Please by D.H. Lawrence

Answer (i) is simply too short to be truly effective. Each sentence contributes to the whole, but there is virtually no detail and certainly no development of the points raised. (Grade: F/E.) Answer (ii), by contrast, sustains the viewpoint and voice of Annie, albeit a little unconvincingly at times. Without being too critical, the emotions are fairly simply represented, as in the line 'I hate him but I love him.' (Grade: D/C.)

The Ragged Trousered Philanthropists by Robert Tressell

In these three answers there is again some correlation between length and quality. Answer (i) reveals a clear understanding of the task and represents accurately, though generally, the pressure of the situation from Jack Linden's point of view. There is, however, little development of feelings and character. (Grade: E/D.) Answer (ii) is much better on the coverage of detail – several of Jack Linden's workmates are mentioned by name and there is more of a sense of narrative. (Grade: C/B.) Answer (iii), however, not only exceeds the others in coverage of detail and depth of character, but it reaches out to an understanding of the wider injustice and also the potential tragedy of Jack Linden's situation. (Grade: A/A*.)

Cold Comfort Farm by Stella Gibbons

Answer (i) is on-task at the start (and the reference to e-mail can be forgiven!), but there is not much of Flora's strength of character emerging. The narrative is tracked for a while, but there is no mention of Judith at all, which is rather a significant omission in a response that is generally quite hesitant. (Grade: E/D.) Answer (ii) contains a rather generous interpretation of Adam as 'kind', but generally there is a more advanced sense of the context than in answer (i). The second half of the answer just explores the situation of Flora's unease a little, though opportunities to make it more convincing are missed. (Grade: C/B.) Answer (iii) picks up Flora's doubts from the start and develops them with some skill. It is a thorough response, one that repeatedly uses narrative details (inserting them seamlessly into the flow) and one that maintains the sense of Flora putting on a brave face. (Grade: A/A*.)

Extraordinary Little Cough by Dylan Thomas

Answer (i) pays the penalty for loose reading and perhaps not taking this empathy question seriously. The general situation is understood, for Jean is clearly living her romance to the full, but there is none of the detail to distinguish Dylan and Brazell. The reference to feelings for George confirms a hit-and-miss approach to the task. (Grade: E/D.) In answer (ii) there is an early (if unsubtle!) reference to Jean's confident personality, followed by a clear understanding (from Jean's perspective) of the rivalry between Dylan and Brazell. There is some sensible selection of detail. (Grade: C/B.) Answer (iii), however, is more thorough and could be said to explore some of the details with confidence. The character of Jean emerges as less of a caricature in this answer. (Grade: B/A.)

Extension work on prose reading

Using the text – extending the questions

The longer texts in Section 1 of the *Students' Book* are comparable in length with passages of prose literature used in Section A of Paper 1. Below are examples of questions that could be used for fuller work on the passages.

Foundation Tier questions

Passage from *The Ragged Trousered Philanthropists* (see *Students' Book*, pages 36–7; Question 4 below also appears in the *Students' Book*).

Look at lines 1 to 12 (up to '... even when we're busy.')

1. **What are your thoughts and feelings about the behaviour of Misery?** (10 marks)

Now look at lines 13 to 24 (up to '... hold the pumice stone.')

2. **What are Jack Linden's reactions to Misery in these lines? Refer closely to the text in your answer.** (10 marks)

Look at lines 25 to the end.

3. **How does the writer make these lines tense and dramatic?** (10 marks)

You should consider:

♣ what happens in these lines
♣ the writer's choice of words
♣ anything else about the way the passage is written.

To answer the next question, consider the passage as a whole.

4. **Imagine you are Jack Linden. At home you tell your wife about the events of the day at work.** (10 marks)

Higher Tier questions

Passage from *On the Black Hill* (see *Students' Book*, pages 20–21)

Look at lines 1–10 (up to ' ... and the Major, also, sat down.')

1. **What are your thoughts and feelings as you read these lines? How does the writer create these thoughts and feelings?** (10 marks)

Now look at lines 11–30 (up to '... to do his duty ...')

2. **How does the writer present Colonel Bickerton?** (10 marks)

Look at lines 31–42 (up to 'Suddenly, you could hear a pin drop.')

3. **How does the crowd react to Colonel Bickerton? Refer closely to the text in your answer.** (10 marks)

Look at lines 43 to the end.

4. **How effective is the ending of the passage?** (10 marks)

Think about:

♣ the feelings you experience as you read these lines
♣ the mood and atmosphere
♣ the writer's technique and use of language.

NOTE There is no definitive difference between Foundation Tier and Higher Tier texts and questions, but there is likely to be a recognizable gradient of demand between the two tiers.

Section 2: Descriptive and imaginative writing

Introduction

Section B of English Paper 1 tests the skills of writing by setting a compulsory descriptive writing task, followed by a piece of imaginative writing selected from a list of five or six straightforward prompts. Student responses are judged against two broad sets of criteria:

♠ *content and form* – accounting for the greater part of the weighting
♠ *sentence structure, punctuation and spelling* – the lesser part of the weighting but intrinsic to the overall success of any piece of writing.

These criteria are covered in the second section of the *Students' Book* within three units:

2.1 Writing to *inform, explain, describe* (descriptive writing – a sense of place)
2.2 Writing to *explore, imagine, entertain* (imaginative writing – narratives)
2.3 Technical accuracy in descriptive and imaginative writing.

The descriptive writing instruction may be seen as a 'set-piece' writing task, but students should aim to write in a way that does not fall into the trap of cliché and stereotype. They should attempt to write with a sense of purpose, realism and individual insight, rather than to a template of predictable images.

The imaginative writing task puts a degree of emphasis on the personal maturity of the student – a silly, juvenile response to a writing prompt will not win due respect from the examiner. There are several examples in the following pages of responses where the student has not been thoughtful enough in organizing a narrative. Put simply, students should apply the same critical standards to their own writing as they would to others.

Technical accuracy ('sentence structure, punctuation and spelling') is judged alongside 'content and organization' in the assessment of writing. Within reason, errors in writing are tolerated in even the best papers, particularly where a student is ambitious in style and in the use of vocabulary. Careless errors are costly, however – not only in terms of reduced credit in examinations, but also in terms of time spent in diagnosis and remedial action.

Two answers are given for each of the tasks in this section. Comments on the responses are included at the end of each unit. The responses were written by GCSE students in roughly the 25 minutes (descriptive writing) and 40 minutes (imaginative writing – narrative) that would be allocated to a single writing task in the exam. Teachers might wish to follow this principle when using the *Students' Book* – students discuss and plan to 'a state of readiness', then answer the question 'against the clock'.

Mark scheme for descriptive writing

Descriptive writing pieces should be assessed by making best-fit judgements across and within the broad grade bands. In 'best-fit' judgements, weaknesses in some areas are compensated by strengths in others. For practical purposes, students could be advised to consider *content and organization* first, then to confirm or refine judgements by considering *sentence structure, punctuation and spelling.*

Content and organization	Sentence structure, punctuation and spelling
G/F ♣ Some relevant content, uneven coverage ♣ Some features of organization or form ♣ Paragraphs may be used to group ideas ♣ Some appropriate detail at a general level ♣ Limited range of vocabulary	**G/F** ♣ Mostly simple or compound sentences ♣ Conjunctions such as 'and' or 'so' ♣ Punctuation attempted where appropriate ♣ Simple spellings usually accurate ♣ Uneven control of verb tense and agreement
E/D ♣ Content attempts to interest the reader ♣ Writing mostly organized appropriately ♣ Paragraphs logically ordered and sequenced ♣ Some attempt to focus on particular details ♣ Some range and selection of vocabulary	**E/D** ♣ Varied sentences, compound and complex used ♣ Some subordination for clarity ♣ Some control of range of punctuation ♣ Simple polysyllabic spellings usually accurate ♣ Generally secure control of tense and agreement
C/B ♣ Relevant, coherent, engaging, sustained content ♣ Writing organized in an appropriate form ♣ Paragraphs used consciously for structure ♣ Well organized, detailed content ♣ Effective range of vocabulary	**C/B** ♣ Range of structures, varied sentence length/focus ♣ Effective simple, compound, complex sentences ♣ Effective, accurate range of punctuation ♣ Most spelling correct, including irregular words ♣ Secure control of tense and agreement
A/A* ♣ Well judged, sustained, pertinent content ♣ Well crafted, structured, stylish writing ♣ Effective, varied, controlled paragraphs ♣ Sophisticated organization of detailed content ♣ Wide range of appropriate, ambitious vocabulary	**A/A*** ♣ Effective variation of sentence structures ♣ Sophisticated, effective use of a range of sentences ♣ Accurate punctuation for deliberate effects ♣ Correct spelling, including complex irregular words ♣ Confident, purposeful tense changes

Unit 2.1 Writing to inform, explain, describe

A sense of place

♣ **Write a description of a funfair.**

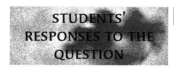
STUDENTS'
RESPONSES TO THE
QUESTION

i

The bright lights of the 'Sizzler' mirrored the starry sky.

'Do you want to go faster?' Screams replied. Spinning round, twisting, turning and tumbling. The smell of the hot-dogs and burgers surrounding the whole place. The siren of the bumper cars sounding every five minutes. Bang, crash, boom.

Your reflection in the hall of mirrors. Shorter, fatter, thinner. Your face lengthens. Your legs shorten. You're unrecognisable! You're still dizzy from the 'Sizzler'.

Everyone tries to squeeze onto the same ride, pushing and shoving …

'Fifty pence a ride! Fifty pence a ride!'

The tears run down a young boy's face. 'Why can't I go on that ride, mummy?'

The height sign flashes 'Too short! Too short!'

Red puffy eyes. But the pink fluffy sweetness will make it better. Candy floss. Fluffy like clouds, wrapped in brightly coloured plastic. Always puts a smile on someone's face.

Time has flown. It's the call out for a last ride. Everyone rushes to their favourite ride. Everyone on the 'Thunder Whipper' throws their hands in the air. Multi-coloured seats all filled with bodies jumping up and down in excitement.

ii

It was a winter's night. The moon was shining brightly and stars were gleaming from the black velvet sky. Music could be heard and people screaming with laughter. The funfair had temporarily transformed the car park into a magnificent fair. In every direction that I looked, people were enjoying themselves, squealing with laughter at the prospect of a fun filled night. There were many new and exciting rides to go on.

As I walked further and further into the fair, there was a very strong smell of burgers and hot-dogs which were being purchased from a big blood-red coloured van, decorated with pictures of cartoon-like fast food. To the left of the van stood a small boy, eating a hot dog with tomato ketchup running all down his T-shirt and splattered around his mouth. Suddenly a loud siren had gone off, signalling the end of the ride with many people lining up after exiting to have another go.

As I glanced in the other direction, I noticed another ride, with flashing lights glowing vividly through the thick artificial smoke. The ride's title was glittering in the lights, with the loud bass line of the music playing over the screams from the people on the ride. I stepped forward and felt the strong breeze caused by the terrific speed of the ride. The carts were buzzing past in a blur and in the background was a young boy shouting into the microphone at the people waiting to go on the ride, but his voice was drowned out over the sounds of the music and the screaming laughter.

To the left, a group of girls were giggling with glee at the prospect of testing 'Tropical Fever'. 'Tropical Fever' was a magnificent new ride that had attracted the attention of many people. The ride would lift the passengers up and around in a circle, many times, over and over, faster and faster and faster … until finally safely lowering them back to the ground, where they stumbled dizzy and turning green, agreeing that it was the best ride they had ever been on. These passengers then stumbled into the arcade to recover. The machines inside were flashing 'Big Win' and '£££££', beckoning passers by to enter. The machines buzzed and shook and whirred and occasionally paid out a stack of ten pence pieces, with a metallic clatter. Then the winnings, no matter how big or small, were inevitably replayed into the machines, forcing the players to leave with lighter pockets than when they entered.

As I began to walk out of the car park, I passed many other people and I thought to myself what an overwhelming experience a fair is.

♣ **Describe the scene in a park on a summer's day.**

It was a beautiful summer's day and I had gone for a walk into the park. I took a seat on an old wooden bench, which had old planks of wood, which had been broken, and somehow repaired very untidily. The birds were singing very loudly in the trees, and there were children and parents playing together in the park like one big happy family, kicking footballs, playing cricket, they even had a little picnic, which they were currently eating, and by the looks of it were enjoying very much.

The lake had small waves rippling through it, where the swans and ducks had been flapping their wings to try and glide along the river, to get nearer the droplets of bread which had been deposited into the river by small children.

The smell of sizzling sausages coming from the stall over by the swings was tremendous, and made my stomach rumble, as I hadn't had my breakfast, and this smell was making me really hungry. The sound of children laughing and screaming could be heard all around the park, some having the time of their lives on the slides, others on the swings.

ii They call it Magic Kingdom. I call it torture. They say that the magic never ends but as I look around I can only see that the queuing never ends. There are people in curling and zigzagging lines, crushed together and restraining bored children from escaping. The noise is brutal. Sweet, sugary Disney songs burn at your ears and bring bile to your throat. Mickey Mouse and Minnie Mouse march beneath the American flag and spout American propaganda to the millions of gullible people lured to this tasteless American Theme Park.

The theme park is consumerism gone mad. There are shops everywhere, where little girls can buy Snow White's dress or Cinderella's Ball Gown for eighty dollars. On every corner is a stand selling hot dogs or cakes, at grossly inflated prices. People line up for everything. There are queues for ice cream, queues for drinks, queues for rides and people just mill about joining one queue and then another in a quest for the ultimate theme park experience.

Hordes of people go to visit Mickey's House, where inanimate objects come strangely to life and spout more Disney songs at the push of a button. The never-ending line grows bigger and bigger, never diminishing, as more people join the queue to have a photo with Mickey Mouse. Behind the secret doors, where the next in line gets to meet this ambassador of America, stand four sweaty humans dressed in identical Mickey Mouse costumes, but secreted away in different compartments lest a tourist should spy this facade, and the great dream becomes shattered for them forever.

People. People. People. Tall, short, thin, fat. Every culture, every ethnic origin and cultural diversity joined together exploring a profit making myth. Men, women and children being robbed of their hard-earned savings in the name of the greatest theme park adventure in the world. Exploitation which is legal.

Rides reach to the sky. Ice cream melts to the floor. Money melts in the pocket. Children cry with exhaustion. Mothers worry about the bills on their mat at home, and fathers bend under the weight of the babies they carry. More people than you can ever imagine are at this legend of a theme park. Heat, sweat, exhaustion, dollars, dollars and more dollars. The incredible consumerism in this incredible adventure of fake dreams.

I survey this scene of madness and find repulsion in my own part in this dynasty of theft. There is nowhere in the world quite like it. The crowds, the sweltering heat, the gaudy images and the heavily costumed actors, are all participating in the magical world of Disney, where the queuing never stops.

♠ Describe the scene in a large shopping centre on Christmas Eve.

i It was Christmas Eve, the snow outside was growing, I was holding my mum's hand walking towards the shopping centre. My mum pushed the clear glass door. Inside were lots of big people like my mum, in the centre of the shops was a big Christmas tree, which grabed my eye it had big shiny bobles and sparkly tinsel. There was a large speaker playing Christmas song which made everyone happy also there was a santas groto with two green elves outside and lots of children waiting to see santa all with smiles on their faces. On the roof were huge flashing lights some were pink some were blue they just beamed down on everybody. Shops had colourful Christmas decorations in the windows everyone was in the Christmas spirit, it was bright and decorated carefully seeing as it was a incredibly big place. When we came out of the centre it made me feel like Christmas was really here.

ii *The shopping centre was brimming with people doing last minute shopping. Everywhere you turned you'd bump into someone as it was so busy. Young children watched eagerly the beautiful, well thought out Christmas decorations. Wonderful. This is the only word that could describe them. From red and gold to silver and blue, the colours of the decorations, these were one of the main attractions in the centre. The sparkling fairy lights brightened up the place, with the lights on the ceiling shining down on the cold, stone flooring, making the place seem magical. All of the shops were Christmassy and the counter staff were more helpful than ever. The workers gleamed with happiness and were so jolly that coming from each shop made you feel happy at this special time of year.*

There were bells, Christmas trees, presents and sleighs dangling above our heads on the ceilings, big and small. Christmas shops, big they were too, were jam-packed full of Christmas cheer, ranging from gift bags to Christmas trees, taking up most of the spare outlets in the mall. A magical point for the children and the young-at-heart was Santa's grotto. Lined with metres upon metres of artificial snow, reindeer and Santa's helpers, the grotto was a make-believe place for children. The orderly queue was kept in line by the helpers and each child spent a good five minutes meeting Santa. They came out starry-eyed and each one with a present, their day seemed fulfilled!

The shopping mall, with over 300 shops, seemed completely festive because of all of the activities going on. For the children there was face painting, their favourite Christmas characters, a colouring corner, a bouncy castle and an opportunity to have your photo taken with the reindeers. And for the adults, there was a skating rink outside and mulled wine and minced pies. You couldn't have asked for a better day out, the day before Christmas.

The centrepiece of the mall was undoubtedly the Christmas Tree. Gigantic and proud it stood in the centre, taking the spotlights from all of the other wonders. Decorated marvellously in blue and silver, with its five thousand fairy lights and goodness knows how many strands of silver braids covering the alpine tree. It made you think 'Wow' and made you stop to think about how well the beautiful tree was planned out.

The toyshops were overflowing with parents and children rushing out to get the latest 'must-haves' and it looked as if it would take hours to pick up all of the toys that had fallen off the shelves.

Unit 2.1 Comments on the student responses

A sense of place

Description of a funfair

Answer (i) expresses the atmosphere of a funfair quite well. The style is unconventional and imaginative. It would be harsh not to appreciate the effort to create a sense of immediacy – in this case it helps to convey the chaos and noise at a typical funfair. This response is fairly short but action and dialogue are nicely mixed. There is, though, some uncertainty with tenses and some overuse of minor sentences. C grade qualities, not entirely secure.

Answer (ii) is a well thought out response with consideration given to each of the five senses. This answer also manages to capture the atmosphere of being in a funfair. There are a few particularly good touches in this response, including the description of the arcade machines and the description of the people on the rides. On the whole, it is a very competent, if rather conventional piece. The sustained accuracy and thorough content take this into the A/A* range. There may be scope for extra touches of style and vocabulary, but this piece stands as an accomplished examination response.

Description of a park on a summer's day

Answer (i) offers a good description. The park is busy and the descriptions of all the people playing games help to convey the idea that there is much to see. This student has tried hard to think of different aspects of the park and attention is paid to each of the senses. The addition of personal details and emotions makes the description come to life, 'made my stomach rumble, as I hadn't had my breakfast'. This piece is a little short, however, and occasionally the punctuation is loose. The first paragraph particularly ends with a lack of control. It was a good idea to create an eye-witness effect by using the first-person 'I', but the images are rather idealized and general. The reliable expression would probably take this into C grade, but no higher.

Answer (ii) is outstanding. It is perhaps intimidating to many students, because they might feel that such a standard is for them unattainable, but there are several qualities that can be noted. Firstly, the piece is clearly from the heart of someone who has 'lived the experience'. It is a particular description, rather than a generalized one. The critical viewpoint is perfectly valid as an ingredient of descriptive writing, and it is controlled and interwoven with the descriptive details. The picture is alive with the participants and the critic is part of the scene too. It deserves the highest praise and the highest possible grade.

Description of a shopping centre on Christmas Eve

Neither of these answers is particularly realistic, with everyone being excited and relaxed and happy. This is almost certainly not accurate for people shopping the day before Christmas. It is usually chaotic and the shoppers are aggressive and selfish rather than 'full of the Christmas spirit'! However, the limitation of the first answer goes beyond that criticism to the weaknesses in spelling, sentence structure and punctuation. Set against this, the child's point of view is a clever feature, to some extent explaining the idealized description. Overall, the response is somewhat lightweight in content and expression and would probably not quite achieve a mark in the C/B grade band. Answer (ii) is a much more developed response and this student has focused on a wide range of aspects of the shopping centre. The writing is mature and well thought out and mistakes are rare. Certainly the quality of the description firmly overrides any criticism of the unrealistic portrayal of the scene. It should command a mark in the A/A* grade band.

Mark scheme for imaginative writing

Imaginative writing pieces should be assessed by making best-fit judgements across and within the broad grade bands. In 'best-fit' judgements, weaknesses in some areas are compensated by strengths in others. For practical purposes, students could be advised to consider content and organization first, then to confirm or refine judgements by considering sentence structure, punctuation and spelling.

Content and organization	Sentence structure, punctuation and spelling
G/F ♣ Basic sense of plot and characterization ♣ Simple chronological writing ♣ Content of narratives may be undeveloped ♣ Paragraphs group ideas into some order and space ♣ Limited range of vocabulary	**G/F** ♣ Mostly simple or compound sentences ♣ Conjunctions such as 'and' or 'so' ♣ Punctuation attempted where appropriate ♣ Simple spellings usually accurate ♣ Uneven control of verb tense and agreement
E/D ♣ Some control of plot and characterization ♣ Some conscious construction of narrative ♣ Appropriate beginning and conclusion ♣ Narrative developed to engage the reader ♣ Paragraphs logically ordered and sequenced ♣ Some range of vocabulary, creating some effect	**E/D** ♣ Varied sentences, compound and complex used ♣ Some subordination for clarity ♣ Some control of range of punctuation ♣ Simple polysyllabic spellings are usually accurate ♣ Generally secure control of tense and agreement
C/B ♣ Writing controlled and coherent ♣ Plot and characterization convincingly sustained ♣ Narrative organized and sequenced purposefully ♣ Engaging narrative with shape, pace and detail ♣ Detailed content is well organized ♣ Varied paragraphs linked by connectives ♣ Some use of devices to achieve particular effects ♣ Effective and precise range of vocabulary	**C/B** ♣ Range of structures, varied sentence length/ focus ♣ Effective simple, compound, complex sentences ♣ Effective, accurate range of punctuation ♣ Most spelling correct, including irregular words ♣ Secure control of tense and agreement
A/A* ♣ Writing with originality and imagination ♣ Plot and characterization convincingly constructed ♣ Material prioritized to maintain interest ♣ Narrative purposeful, sequenced, well paced ♣ Paragraphs varied, structured, controlled ♣ Cohesion reinforced with connectives/links ♣ Conscious and effective use of devices ♣ Effective, precise, ambitious vocabulary	**A/A*** ♣ Effective variation of sentence structures ♣ Sophisticated, effective use of range of sentences ♣ Accurate punctuation for deliberate effects ♣ Correct spelling, including complex irregular words ♣ Confident, purposeful tense changes

Unit 2.2 Writing to explore, imagine, entertain

Narratives

♣ **Write about a time when you felt very surprised.**

STUDENTS' RESPONSES TO THE QUESTION

i

It was around about April when my oldest sister Sam told me that she was pregnant. At first I thort that she was joking but when I looked at her face I could tell that she was telling the truth. She looked so happy and with her husband Paul siting next to each other thay looked so happy and they looked like a perfect copal. My sister had her hand on her stumuck and that maid me feel so happy fore them it was grait. I was not ready fore my sister to say anything like that I was so surprised.

But then my sister said that there was even more of a surprise. I thort that nothing could get much beter than that. But then shey said that she was having twins. I could not bolive it I was shockt because there will be two new babys in the family, and my family already had twins in there it was Sam and Helen. One of the twins are having more twins. My family was already big but with two new babys in the family my family is just geting biger and biger. That night I kept on looking at my sisters stumuck I could not bolive it when they left I went to bed. I could not stop thinking about them. I was thinking wat would thay be, wat thay would look like, and wat thay would call me.

ii

It was a sunny Sunday afternoon in the summer. I was fishing down at the lake just south of Roswell. I was fishing for trout at the time I had already cought three of a nice sise as well. I fell asleep at about one o'clock and I was woken up by a large explosion. I could see smoke rising over the hill on the other side of the lake. So I whent to investigate. I got there, there was a large black crater, It had been burnt, at the bottom of the crater there was a large object looked like a space ship with aliens. I was so scared I ran back to town, to my mam and Dad. I was only nine at the time. They didn't believe me. They said, 'Look son it was probibly one of your Dreams again.'

But it wasn't, so I got my friends and my friend he had a gun only an air rifle but it made us all feel a bit safer. We got to the crater we could here voices and see people moving around in white uniforms like scientists in the movies. Then we were cought by men in black suits I screamed and screamed more than I had eva done in my life before. With seeing the aliens in the crater and now this. 'And that's what I saw sir.' I answered the Agent.

'Well these aliens that you saw where in fact people and the space ship is part of the US government. Thank you for your statement sonny. That will be all, you can go home now.' The agent said.

Extension work

Discuss these responses. Comment on their strengths and weaknesses. Identify and correct the errors in the writing.

♣ **Write [the opening paragraph for] a story based on the title: 'The visit'.**

STUDENTS' RESPONSES TO THE QUESTION

i

I was at home on the 30th of October when I was just sitting on the sofa and the phone rang. I was the only one in the house at the time dad was at work and mum was out in the garden planting flowers. I got up and answered the phone. There was a quite funny quint voise and the person said 'Come to the front door and open it. Then you will see a big Yamaha motacross wagen parked the opisit side of the road go over and open the side door and come in' and then he put the phone down so I put my shoes on opened the front door and looked, there it was. The big Yamaha motacross wagen had Yamaha racing across it and it was dark blue and on the back there was 426 cc 4 stroke on a trailer. I went over opened the door and went in. I couldn't bleve it, it was my best friend Joe Newbold from my old school 'I said what you doing here' he said he'd come to visit me and that we were going to the APEX track down the road. His older brother was there to Tom we loaded my Yamaha 250 cc 4 stroke onto the trailer and set of we had a brillant day when we got back we went in the house had some tea and then Joe had to go so we arranged for him to come again and we'd keep in touch and then he went home.

ii It was summer last year and my mum and dad asked me,
'Trudy, where would you like to go on holiday this year?'
'Is it alright to go to North Yorkshire? Jess said that there is lots of things there to go and see!'
'Well, lets have a look how much it is, calculate it up mum for the three of us to go there!' Dad asked mum politely.
'Tommy it costs up to £350 and we'll need to take spare money and petrol money that's another £150, that's a bit too expensive Trudy, can't we take you to Pontins holiday park it is much cheaper and it is near us!' Mum made a large sacrifice that we would never go to a holiday park again!
'Please dad can we go if I pay for some of it with my pocket money!' I sounded desperate.
'OK then I suppose we can go there, Trudy, you had better start packing because we will be leaving next week!' Dad said to Trudy.
'Yes! Thank you very much Dad, thanks mum, I love you both very much!' I said gracefully to mum and dad.
'Mum, how long are we going for?' Trudy asked mum politely.
'About two weeks, but pack up to three weeks of clothes because you might get the other ones wet!' Mum said.
'OK, thanks mum' Trudy said and walked back into her bedroom.
Trudy, mum and dad are near Scarborough and Trudy is really bored and then asks repetively 'Dad are we there yet? I'm bored.' I ask my dad.
'No Trudy now stop asking, read your magazine or do your cross stitch or even go to sleep!' Dad shouted at me again. I think he is very agitated and he wants to turn back, but I wanted to carry on but dad really wanted to turn round so he did! The fun about this holiday was that I enjoyed the journey up and back, but I don't care I enjoyed it a lot.

Extension work

Discuss different ways of responding to the title 'The Visit'. Suggest how the answers above might have focused more successfully on the task.

♣ **Write [the opening paragraph of] a story in response to: 'Write about a time when you took part in sport.'**

i

At the designated starting point the other competitors were milling about eagerly waiting for the off. The sight of all these other athletes made me wonder whether I was fit enough to compete with them and their superior bicycles. The time had come and the riders were now lining up across the road ready for the starter's gun to signal the beginning of the race. My heart was now beating at a fast pace in anticipation and my mouth was now dry. I took my place in the line and the starter called out 'On your marks. Get set,' and fired the gun, at the same time as stepping smartly out of the way.

All the riders started off slowly at first and then as we picked up speed they began to string out along the route. It appeared that I was about half way along the group but making progress with every turn of the pedals. I was passing rider after rider. Excitement now took over from the apprehension I had felt earlier, before the race had begun. Uphill and down the other side, across long flat winding roads and back up another hill and I was still picking off the occasional rival.

A few miles from the finish and I was now concentrating hard on my breathing and pedalling. Now in the first group of five cyclists the pace was heating up and I was feeling exillerated at the prospect of the end of the race. Around the last turn for home and the final sprint had began. Getting out of the saddle and pedalling for all my worth, I could see the white finish line tape in the distance.

We crossed the line in a bunch and after stopping some distance beyond I collapsed over the handlebars, my heart thumping like a drum. As I calmed down I congratulated myself on a fine finish in third place, resolving to do better next time.

ii I stood at the very edge of the pool, dressed in a shirt and a skirt with my swimming costume on underneath. I waited for the signal from the examiner and to keep calm I focused my eyes on the far end of the pool. This was not a race. There were no competitors on either side of me. I stood alone above the clear gently rippling water. My only competitor was time. I had to beat the clock. What if I didn't make it? My heart rate began to increase. What if I was too slow? What if I pushed myself too hard and I got tired? I could feel my pulse throbbing rapidly in my temple. What if I swallowed too much water in the rush? What if . . .? But then the examiner had blown her whistle and all of those fears had vanished from my mind. Unbutton the shirt. Unbutton the skirt. Now dive.

I dived into the water, cutting through it like a torpedo. I opened my eyes and in a watery blur I could just make out the dark blue tiles lining the far wall of the pool. I surfaced and began kicking with all my strength. My long legs stretched out far behind me, and my arms pulled fiercely at the water ahead. I tried to focus on my breathing and nothing else. Nearly there. A few more strokes. Keep going. Breathe. Breathe. Breathe.

I touched the far wall of the pool and spun around in the water, so I was facing back up towards the deep end. I pushed off with all my might from the wall behind me to give me a head start for the return swim. I kicked and kicked. The muscles in my legs began screaming in agony. The pulse in my temple began throbbing again and I lost my concentration. I breathed out hard and breathed in deeply. With the oxygen I took in huge gulps of water. I began spluttering and choking. My eyes began to water and my throat felt blocked. I was only a few metres away from the wall. My feet began sinking towards the floor in response to the stress I was feeling. I could hear my friends cheering me on from the side of the pool. I stretched out with my fingers. The wall was just beyond my reach. One more kick. Just one more kick. My head felt light and it felt like there was no air in my lungs at all. Just one more kick. My legs and arms were shaking and I reached out. I feel the smooth coldness of the tile underneath my fingertips. I'd made it. Just.

♣ **Write [the opening paragraph to] your own story using the opening line: 'It was my first day at work and I had no idea what to expect …'**

It was my first day at work and I had no idea what to expect. I didn't know any body and I didn't know if I could do the job required. Every one was speaking highly off my qualifications but I was worried I would disappoint every one. I always wanted to be a police man but now I have achieved it I don't know what it will be like. I was also worried because I was new and I went up to a higher rank because of my qualifications but would the other officers who had been there for years and were lower ranks get annoyed and give me a hard time.

Another thing I was concerned about was the things I heared about police men and women getting badly hurt in the act of duty. My main wory was the fact that my dad was in the police force and he got beaten up in a dark alley and was left for dead, I think to myself could this happen to me. I also felt like I was betraying my family because they were dead against me joining the police after what happened to my dad and all the pain they went through.

I didn't know what to say or do when I got to the station I felt very nervous and vunerouble to all the other police men and women that would be there. I was still considering whether I would turn up for the job or whether I would ring up and say I couldn't do it. I had to pick between a good salary or family loyalty. I would have got over it in the end so I went to work and my family understood why so they supported me.

On the first day not mainy people spoke to me But as the days went on more and more people started speaking to me. I was happy and I was also wrong to fear the fact of working in a police station.

ii It was my first day at work and I didn't know what to expect. I got up out of bed and I looked out the window the sun was shining bright as it normally did. I got dressed in my new suit ready for my new job but I didn't know what to expect anything could happen on my first day. I left my house early so I would be on time as it was my first day. I got to the place I was working it was in an office which I thought was big. I went to my bosses office and he showed me around, then he showed me to my desk. It was big with a computer on it. I thought to myself I'm going to like it here but that was until I got a pile of paper work on my desk to put in order, to write letters and to put them in the filing cabinet. I didn't expect this at all. I did this all day. I thought I would get something exciting to do.

It was about three o'clock and I finished typing letter, filing all the work and putting it in order. I walked over to my bosses office and I asked him 'Is there any more filing you want me to do?' and he said to me 'That was a test to see if you can cope under pressure with lots of paper work and you certainly proved that to me.' 'You were watching me all day?' I asked. 'Yes and I'm very prode not all my workers can cope, now you know what to expect on your first day at work.' Said my boss. 'Yes' I replied. The days I was there I certainly knew what to expect.

Extension work

Discuss the limitations of the pieces of writing above. Correct the errors and suggest improvements to the style and structure of each piece.

♣ **Write [the final paragraph for] a story that ends with the line:**
'... **He picked up his bag and walked away without looking back.**'

It's a cold windy night and again I'm looking for a place to sleep. Everywhere I look, in the doorways, by the bins, on the pavements, I see them. Old people, young people, small and big people — littering the place up, so they say.

'Hi' I said 'You been on the streets long?' He looks quite new, he looks normal. His hair was short brown and shiney, he looked clean, hardly a dirt patch on him.

'It's my first day, my parents kicked me out. They said I was a bad influence on my family. I'm not that bad, 17 and been to jail twice.'

'What for?'

'Stealing basically. How long have you been on the streets?'

'Couple of years now. Each day goes past and it gets no easier. I mean living on the streets is bad, but when people like you the new ones come along and steal our places in a good sheltered place it gets worse. Having no money and begging is bad. Rich people couldn't care less about us.'

'What do you mean?'

'We go round asking for money to get a little bite, and they believe we are only asking for money to get back on a drug addiction. We've got to face the facts no matter how hard we try we'll never have a proper job, get a house, nothing unless our families or friends let us move back in and give us a second chance'.

'You mean never?'

'Why do you think so many of the people round here are old, skinny and dirty. There might be rare chance that you do get off the streets but it's very slim.'

'I never thought.'

'People never do when they begin living on the streets until its to late.'

He looked at me and sighed, 'You know what I'm going to go back to my parents and ask for a second chance.'

'It might not be easy. I know my parents wouldn't.'

'You don't know my parents. They already offered me a second chance. I turned them down. I wanted to be free, live without them. You know. Thanks mate. You've really helped me.'

'What have I done?'

'Opened my eyes.'

'I'm only being realistic.'

He looked at me and smiled. He picked up his bag and walked away without looking back.

ii Its over. There's no way we can continue our relationship if I can't trust him to stay faithful. No, not even faithful but truthful. The lies he comes out with, when I know too well what he's been up to. He must think I'm some child who you can lie to to make life easier. Well, I'm not going to put up with it any longer. That was the plan – to finish with him and to send him away with his bags packed and waiting by the front door. Although, as with most of my plans, it didn't go how I'd expected. Here's what happened. He left for work at eight thirty, taking with him the tuna sandwich I'd already prepared and his black briefcase that makes him look more qualified than he actually is, giving me a quick peck on the cheek as he passed through the porch.

'See you later babe. Oh, I might be home a bit later tonight, I've got tons of paperwork to catch up on.' He called as he got into the black BMW. It wasn't our car, no, we couldn't afford anything like that, which makes you wonder where all his wages go, because I know for a fact that I don't spend them. But anyway, he'd been using that excuse for a while now so I called back, 'More paperwork? Well don't be too late, I'm going to make you a nice meal tonight. I've got a few things I want to talk about with you.'

'Yeah, whatever you say love' was his reply, which was another indicator that this extra paperwork was actually extra pleasure work. I knew he didn't care if I was putting all my energy into making him a meal. Or, maybe it just didn't sink in, in one ear and out the other as my mother used to say. His mind was always elsewhere these days.

I wasn't going to spend precious time today slaving over a stove. Instead, I spent most of the day sorting out and packing all his clothes for him, he wouldn't want the hassle of that after I'd just told him to leave. At least then he couldn't say I never do anything for him.

At about four thirty I ordered a Chinese takeaway. I dished up, lit the four candles on the table and poured two glasses of wine. From then on it was easy, my preparations were finished and all I had to do was sit and wait. At five minutes to ten I heard his key turn in the lock. I sat down at the table and by this time the candles has nearly run out of wax and the food was stone cold. As he walked through the door he shouted, 'I'm sorry I'm late. I didn't realise I had so much to do.'

'Yeah, well you never do these days.'

'What do you mean? What was it you wanted to talk about?'

'I think you've got some explaining to do.'

'Look, I said I'm sorry.'

'No, I mean your bit on the side.'

'What, I don't know what your talking about. Linzie, she's just a work colleague.'

'Oh, so that's what you call them. I'm sorry, I can't go on like this. I think you should leave.'

He said nothing and I don't think he was too bothered because he picked up his bag and walked away without looking back.

Unit 2.2 Comments on the student responses

Narratives

A time you felt very surprised

Answer (i) is a narrative based on a real life experience of the student. Because of this the student is able to comment throughout the story on the emotions experienced during this surprising event. This makes the passage come to life and it is interesting for the reader. However, the poor punctuation and spelling make it difficult to understand on occasions and this detracts from the story quite significantly. The story is not well developed – time could have been spent expanding on some of the events and dialogue could have been added to make the passage more enjoyable. E/F qualities dominate.

Answer (ii) tries a contrasting approach with an aliens story. In this answer, though, the topic is not handled with any conviction. There is a promising attempt to include dialogue, but sentence structure needs to be varied for the interest of the reader and some descriptive detail incorporated. The ending works only in a simple way, as a punchline. Overall the piece is of E/F quality.

The visit

Answer (i) is not clearly focused on the task of the visit. Instead, this student seems keen to demonstrate his/her knowledge of Yamaha motorbikes! This does detract from the story, and potentially narrows the audience to the specialist. Poor spelling and punctuation further impair this response. The control that is evident at the start of the piece is lost as the story develops. More attention needs to be paid here to the structure of the story and the needs of the reader. The story just retains a place in the D/E band despite the deterioration.

Answer (ii) is arguably more about a journey than a visit and so does raise the issue as to how this piece should be viewed for content. In addition to this, the narration switches repeatedly from first person to third person. This makes for some confusion. In fairness, as this a piece of open writing, the title is regarded as a touchstone for imagination as well as a focus for structure. This student therefore would not be penalized for her interpretation of the title, but she has missed an opportunity to write a more structured story. The writing though is engaging and bright and it would earn a mark in the D/E grade band.

A time when you took part in sport

Answer (i) captures the exhilaration of a bicycle race. The use of both short and long sentences helps to convey the anticipation and speed of taking part in a race. There are only occasional spelling and punctuation errors. This is a well thought out piece and the frequent comments about the thoughts of the writer help the reader to picture exactly what is going on and how it feels to be in a race. Very secure in C/B band overall.

Answer (ii) is very similar in many ways to answer (i). This passage also uses short sentences to convey the sense of urgency in the piece. The descriptions of being in the water are very realistic and the use of rhetorical questions at the beginning of the piece involve the reader immediately, because these are questions that the reader is asking of the narrator also. Right up until the final sentence it is not certain whether the narrator will succeed or not and this keeps the reader hanging on every word. The intensity of this sporting experience is significantly greater than in answer (i) and achieved with impressive control. In the grade B/A area, worthy of consideration for grade A.

Narratives built on an opening line

There appears to be C grade potential in answer (i) that is not fulfilled, probably through lack of planning and organization. The new policeman seems extraordinarily nervous about taking up a post, discussing issues that should have been resolved much earlier. So the writing lacks a clear sense of purpose and structure, and technically is limited too. This piece does not convincingly portray the emotions felt when starting a new job – it lacks the ring of truth, in fact. D/E grade band.

Answer (ii) is a little more organized. There is a sense of purpose and some good control of sentences in places. It ends quite well, with a convincing portrayal of the boss and a well defined moment of dialogue. The student has a plain style, but evokes the situation of 'first day' quite successfully. Closer to grade C than answer (i), but inconsistent performance probably keeps this piece in grade D overall.

Narratives leading up to a finishing line

Answer (i) tries to deal with the complex issue of homelessness. There is an imbalance between the amount of dialogue and the amount of action in this story. The dialogue itself is a little bit naïve, but it is at least trying to deliver a positive message and is very coherent and technically sound. The voices do not establish the characters with real credibility, but as mouthpieces they are effective. C grade for a competent, all-round performance, but not in the upper reaches of the C/B band.

Answer (ii) also deals with a sensitive issue, that of infidelity. This piece is quite contradictory in places, with the narrator refusing to cook for her partner, but still prepared to pack his suitcases for him because 'he wouldn't want the hassle of that after I'd just told him to leave'. In all, this is a credible, worldly-wise piece of writing, written with occasional lapses of accuracy and style, but largely sound. There is some credit for ambition in the subject-matter, carried out with some success. Secure in the C/B band.

Extension work on descriptive and imaginative writing

Linking reading with writing – exploring techniques

The piece below is an exceptional response to the imaginative writing prompt: 'I had never liked mobile phones and now I knew why ...' The questions that follow it are 'borrowed' from Section A of Paper 1 to reinforce the link between reading and writing on this paper. It is an analytical exercise that could be carried out in class on any successful piece of exam or coursework writing.

I had never liked mobile phones and now I knew why. A while ago now, my older (supposedly wiser) brother gave me his old mobile phone because he'd got a new fancy one, with an internet connection and all these irritating ringtones, which sounded absolutely nothing like the tunes they were supposed to be, and about fifty million different games on it, which all seemed to involve pictures made up of little squares, and the player sitting hunched over, two thumbs tapping away like mad, staring, fixated, at the little screen for hours on end, so, when you tried to speak to them, all you got were grunts and 'look, piss off, alright?'. Plus, this wonderful, advanced piece of technology was about the size of a 50p piece with the keys to match. You had to locate and press each of them with a pinhead before they worked and it got lost in the fluff in the bottom of your pocket. Anyway, you get the picture.

Mobile phones are not my favourite piece of equipment in the world. So, God knows why my brother gave me his in the first place. I tried to say no (I did!) but he forced me to take it, saying 'They're really useful. And you're getting it free'. In the end, I took it off him to shut him up! He does go on a bit sometimes, my brother. Like me, I suppose.

So, here I am, with this mobile phone. It's the size of a brick and just as heavy. It's blue, black and red with keys that stick out for about a centimetre, so you couldn't really miss them. They also glow green as well when you press them and make a noise like a foghorn. So, even if you were completely blind, you'd still be able to hear from the other side of the town. I haven't figured out how to turn the volume down yet, that might be why!

The first time I switched the phone on (after spending about an hour trying to find the right button) something came up on the screen. 'Pin number'. What? I didn't have a clue – I thought pin numbers were for cash machines not mobile phones. I went and asked my brother and he tapped it in for me. He told me that if I went into the Menu and selected phone-something-or-other and then change pin number, I'd be able to change it. So I tried but failed miserably. The display refused to change, however many buttons I pressed and I accidentally switched the phone off again a couple of times. In the end, my brother had to do it for me. I think he was getting a bit fed up of me by this time. He said something about writing me an instruction manual, which I thought would be extremely helpful, but he and his friends just laughed at this. Very confusing!

I finally worked out, after several hours of hard practice, how to work the damned thing and went out to meet my friends. We were going to the cinema to see 'Star Wars'. It was packed in the cinema by the time we got there. Luckily, there were four seats in the middle block about halfway down. We squeezed past everybody and plonked ourselves down. We were surrounded by massive gangs of kids of about eleven or twelve years old, throwing salty popcorn and rustling crisp and sweet bags. They were all chattering away like monkeys, jabbering in some alien language I'd never heard before. There was one podgy kid sitting in the row in front of me, exploring his nose with his finger and then inspecting the contents he'd retrieved before consuming them with very apparent relish, whilst slurping his coke. He seemed completely unaware that he was sitting in a crowded room full of people with nothing better to do than sit and watch everyone else till the film started. The lights then came down and a sudden deathly hush descended. (sounded quite Biblical that, didn't it?)

The film was really good. Loads of brilliant, exciting special effects and a great plotline. About halfway through the film, there was a quiet, really intense scene going on. Everybody was still. Even the fat kid had ceased picking his nose and was gawping at the screen along with everyone else. Suddenly, this loud beeping noise started. Everyone looked in my direction. I thought, 'What are they all looking at?' Then I realised. It was that bleedin' phone! I frantically started to look in the pockets of my jacket, thinking 'Where is it? Where is it?' I found it and, not knowing what else to do, answered it. Guess who? My brother. I told him to piss off and turned the phone off. But the damage was done. Everybody around me was tutting. An employee came and told me to leave the cinema, pointing at the huge, conspicuous signs saying 'No mobile phones', as he escorted me out of the cinema. Needless to say, I was incredibly embarrassed. I didn't speak to my brother for about a week afterwards and, believe me, the phone went straight in the bin.

For discussion or written response:

1. What impressions do you get of the writer and his feelings about mobile phones? (paragraphs 1 and 2)

2. How does the writer create humour in these lines? (paragraphs 3 and 4)

3. What are the writer's reactions in this part of the story? (paragraph 5)

4. How effective do you find the ending to this story? (final paragraph)

Section 3: Non-fiction and media reading

Introduction

Section A of English Paper 2 tests the skills of reading by asking a series of questions on a pair of texts, one categorized as non-fiction, the other as a media text. These skills are covered in the third section of the *Students' Book* within four units:

3.1 Locating details

3.2 Explaining and summarizing

3.3 Analysing persuasive techniques

3.4 Comparing non-fiction and media texts

These units focus on different types of question that are asked in the examination, concentrating on the key features of the questions while recognizing that, in practice, the question types overlap considerably. In the exam, a series of four questions will be asked, but these are by no means likely to be focused in sequence in the way of the four units above. The non-fiction and media texts themselves will always determine the questions worth asking, but students can be assured that the skill areas above will be covered, whatever the wording and sequence of the questions. Candidates are strongly advised to focus on the key words of the question, particularly for the question that requires them to consider both texts.

The texts in Section 3 of the *Students' Book* were selected with audience and purpose in mind as well as content and format. In the first three units, texts are featured individually (as is the case in Paper 2, where only one question from four requires consideration of both the non-fiction and the media text). In the final unit, two pairs of 'full length' linked texts are presented, with two 'comparative' questions for each pair submitted, in order to raise students' awareness of a range of question types.

The amount of support for the students varies within a unit. The first task is always given detailed support to re-state the importance of developing an answer fully. The final task in each unit is presented in a way that requires students to apply independently some of the advice given along the way. All tasks are recognizable as exam-style tasks, but the last one in each unit encourages students to be rigorous in terms of timing and organization. Grids are provided to help students structure some of their answers. However, these can only help to some extent, so they appear occasionally rather than for every task. It is vital that students learn to think for themselves.

Two or three responses are given for each of the tasks in this section. Comments on the responses are included at the end of each unit. The responses were written by GCSE students in roughly the 15 minutes that might be allocated to a single reading question in the exam. Teachers might wish to follow this principle when using the *Students' Book* – students read and discuss to 'a state of readiness', then answer the question 'against the clock'.

Mark scheme

This generalized mark scheme uses phrases that are widely used in WJEC examination marking. Teachers and students can work out in which of these broad bands an answer fits and where within the band it might belong.

Grades

u/G
Nothing attempted or struggles to engage with the question and/or the text.

F
♣ Simple comments with occasional reference to the text.
♣ Unselective copying.
♣ Unsupported assertions.

E/D
♣ Simple comments based on surface features of the text.
♣ Awareness of more straightforward implicit meanings.
♣ Some focus on the question. Some awareness of 'how'.
♣ A simple preference (in comparison) based on appropriate textual detail.

C/B
♣ Appropriate material selected from the text to reach valid, sensible conclusions. Sensible inferences.
♣ Use of language beginning to be addressed. Some grasp of the writer's technique. Sense of shape and overview.
♣ Clear focus on persuasive technique. Effect on intended audience considered.
♣ Valid evaluation (in comparison) based on a range of appropriate textual detail.

A/A*
♣ Valid comments based on a thorough exploration of textual detail.
♣ Use of language addressed as well as content.
♣ Coherent overview with specific detail.
♣ Thorough, perceptive, analytical.
♣ Well-considered evaluation (in comparison) based on analysis of appropriate details from both texts. Sustained, organized comparison.

Unit 3.1 Locating details

NOTE In this unit the skill of locating detail (or 'search and find') is isolated from other skills. The accumulation of points is not directly grade-related so it would be misleading to attribute even an estimated grade to the sample answers. Suffice it to say that all students should be determined to get near maximum marks on such questions.

Alton Towers – Staffordshire Pride

♣ **Name ten things from the article that would attract a visitor especially to Alton Towers.**

STUDENTS' RESPONSES TO THE QUESTION

> **i**
> 1. Congo Rapids
> 2. Runaway Train
> 3. Log flume
> 4. Nemesis
> 5. AIR
> 6. Oblivion
> 7. Black Hole
> 8. Landscaped Gardens
> 9. Coffee shops and restaurants
> 10. Gift shops

> **ii**
> There are many attractions at Alton Towers. These include eleven separate zones each with a different theme. Katanga Canyon is the home of the Congo Rapids and Runaway Train, Merrie England has Log Flume and Tea Cups, and Forbidden Valley has the zero gravity roller coaster Nemesis.

Legoland – built to last!

♣ **According to the advert, what attractions can you expect to see at Legoland?**

STUDENTS' RESPONSES TO THE QUESTION

> **i**
> You can see lots of lego models made from plastic blocks of various sizes. Lego is a popular children's toy. You can see Windsor and Mini-land. There is Lego Explore Land, the home of the Ultimate Challenge. But don't think Lego has its fair share of rides.

ii
1. Pirate Falls
2. Miniland, where you can witness the world in miniature
3. Imagination centre
4. Lego Driving School
5. Flying a hot air balloon, which you can control its speed and height
6. Waterworks
7. Fairy Tale Brook
8. Playtown
9. A choice of four restaurants
10. Shops

The Internet – for and against

♣ **Identify five advantages and five disadvantages of using the Internet.**

 STUDENTS'
RESPONSES TO THE
QUESTION

i
Advantages:
1. Ready access to extensive information
2. Offers information that could aid school work
3. Individuals who work unsociable hours can converse with people all over the world
4. Possible to download music and movies
5. Fast and efficient system of emails

Disadvantages
1. Students can copy work off the Internet and pass it off as their own
2. Some people misuse children's chatrooms and prey on the innocent
3. Illegal transfers of music and movies are endangering the industries
4. Important files can be lost
5. No guarantee that emails will reach their intended recipient.

ii
Information; educational; sending emails; hobby; downloading; copying coursework; downloading is illegal

Operation Christmas Child

♠ **Identify five types of gift that can be sent to the children of Eastern Europe and five types of gift that cannot be sent.**

i

It says that the children need hygiene-based products, such as soap and toothpaste. But it isn't recommended to send any liquid based products, e.g. shampoo. It's OK to send clothes, but they need to be small enough to fit into the box. You can send sweets or lollipops but remember to check the sell by date before putting it into the box, so you shouldn't include crisps, biscuits or cakes. It's fine to send toys, for example a teddy bear or jigsaws, but any toys that are war-related are unacceptable. There isn't any point sending books or toys with complicated instructions because they wouldn't understand English. It's also a good idea to send a photo of yourself and a greeting card.

ii

You can send:
1. Hygiene-based products, such as toothbrushes
2. Clothes such as hats
3. Toys such as teddy bears
4. Small sweets
5. Books with pictures

You cannot send:
1. Liquid-based products, such as shampoo
2. Biscuits or cakes
3. War-related toys
4. Toys with complicated instructions
5. Books full of words

Unit 3.1 Comments on the student responses

Alton Towers – Staffordshire Pride

For these answers, students need to identify ten independent attractions at Alton Towers. Answer (i) has used numbered items. This is a good strategy because students can easily monitor how many attractions they have identified. There is some merit perhaps in giving more than ten attractions but students will not get more than ten marks for this question. Because of the wording of the question, gift shops and restaurants can legitimately be included as things that would attract visitors to the park.

It is harder to identify the attractions listed in answer (ii). There is no clear focus on either detailed attractions or zones. The student has not looked beyond the first paragraph of the text to locate details. They cannot really be rewarded both for zones and the attractions within those zones, so the likely result for this response would be six out of ten: four easy marks dropped.

Legoland – built to last!

Answer (i) is an example of aimless copying and a lack of focus on the question. At best the answer would have made four points and some of those are very general. Mentioning Windsor and Miniland in one phrase is very odd too, suggesting a lack of understanding or a very careless reading.

Answer (ii) is much better. The student has clearly identified ten independent points about Legoland. (The extra descriptions of some of these attractions are not necessary, for example, 'Miniland, where you can witness the world in miniature'.) Since this is only a list of attractions, extra credit is not given for offering descriptions of each. All that is really required is the name of the attraction.

The Internet – for and against

In answer (i) the writer has followed the guidelines in the *Students' Book* and given the answers in two parts. This response is thorough and complete, but some students may be tempted to divide some of the points. For example, 'Illegal transfers of music and movies are endangering the industries' is a valid point, but 'Illegal transfers of music are endangering the industry' and 'Illegal transfers of movies are endangering the industry' would not be acceptable as two different points. There are enough advantages and disadvantages in the passage for students to avoid doing this. It should be emphasized that the points made in response to the question have to be drawn from the passage, not from personal knowledge.

Answer (ii) is not at all satisfactory. Advantages and disadvantages are not clearly distinguished, while all of the points made are suspiciously vague and general. If viewed generously, the answer might be worth two or three marks.

Operation Christmas Child

Answer (i) seems like a full answer, but there are only four things listed that you shouldn't send and six things that you can send. Because of the nature of the question, this does not count as ten points. It specifically asks for five of each, so the maximum available to this student is nine marks. The student gets one mark for stating that you can send hygiene-based products, but does not get any additional marks for expanding on this (toothpaste and soap). Sweets and lollipops would also be classed as one mark rather than two (some would argue that lollipops are sweets).

Answer (ii) is much more accurate and clearly identifies ten things that can and cannot be sent. Again, the examples offered for some of the items are not really necessary, for example, 'Hygiene-based products, such as toothbrushes', but it does confirm that the student has correctly identified the items.

Unit 3.2 Explaining and summarizing

P Plates!

♠ What does the writer say to support the use of P plates in Great Britain?

i

The writer tries to support the use of P Plates by telling us that in other countries they have reduced the amount of accidents that occur between 17 and 19 year olds. It also tells us that only 4% of license holders are 17 to 19 year olds and of these 4%, 10% of all accidents that occur involve them.

The writer also tries to encourage using the P Plates by giving us advice of where to buy them from and by telling us how good they are for other drivers to know that they only just passed their test.

ii

The second paragraph is full of statistics and it warms the readers up for the introduction of the P Plates. The statistics show that new licence holders are involved in 10% of accidents. The third paragraph eases you in to the idea of P Plates. The writer uses the government to side with the P Plates and uses their influences, 'However the government encourages their use'. The writer uses other countries to sell P Plates, 'Spain, France, Finland and Japan'. It makes you feel safer in the fourth paragraph saying, 'restricts drivers to a maximum speed of 45 mph.'

The article is aiming at drivers who have recently passed their test and for parents who have children that have recently passed their test. The article is also aimed at older people who want safer roads. The author uses facts and figures to promote the sale of P Plates.

The author uses 'compulsory' which is a much harder word than 'voluntary', 'seeking views on making them compulsory'. This shows that the system works and that it must be good if they are thinking of making it compulsory.

iii The writer is saying that P Plates are good for safety for young drivers particularly. The article is aimed at people in the late teens who have recently passed their driving test or have been driving legally for a year or less with a full licence. It may also be aimed at people later on in life who did not take their test at a young age. I also believe that the article is also aimed at drivers in general to be aware of any young drivers with or without P Plates. I believe this as the article talks of people who have recently passed their tests and also other drivers who should be aware of young drivers.

I believe that the author is supporting the compulsory use of P Plates in Great Britain because of the frightening statistics stated in the passage. It states that 'in 2000 17–19 year olds made up just 4% of license holders, but were involved in 10% of accidents.' It also states that, 'statistics reveal that you are more likely to have an accident in the first two years of driving than at any other point in your driving career'. The writer believes that P Plates will raise everyone's awareness.

It not only uses factual information like statistics to give you the message, but rhetorical questions, 'So what can you do to ease your way into a long safe driving career?' This not only makes you think but it also answers the question with the relevant information. The information given tells you what they stand for and why so many people use P Plates. It also gives examples of other countries who have made them compulsory, for example, 'Spain, France, Finland and Japan' and the success they are having with the use of P Plates.

Again, it gives statistics of how good the P Plates have been in those countries, 'In Australia, accident rates fell 32% and in Norway 50% were less likely to have an accident'. These figures persuade you to be in support of the P Plates.

P Plates!

POINTS TO CONSIDER	COMMENT
♣ Reasons for using P plates	
♣ Arguments for making P plates compulsory	
♣ Who the article is aimed at	
♣ Use of facts and figures	
♣ References to other countries	

Artificial Reality

♦ **What impressions of reality television shows does the writer of this article create?**

i

The writer doesn't seem to like reality TV shows. He starts off by making sarcastic comments about the contestants. This instantly puts the people who try to get on the shows in a bad light, it makes them seem pathetic. The writer also runs down the celebrities who go on the programs, by calling them 'Y-list celebs'.

The author is trying to tell the reader that reality TV isn't really that popular. He is also saying that it is cheap TV, made by producers who haven't got any new ideas. The author is portraying reality TV shows in a tacky light. He is very sarcastic about it and ends up by saying that reality TV is already scraping the barrel for good TV programmes.

ii

The writer disapproves of reality television shows. He refers to the stars of the shows as 'instantly forgettable wannabes' and 'nobodies'. He criticises 'Celebrity Big Brother' and 'I'm a Celebrity Get Me Out of Here,' calling their participants 'once-famous Z-List celebs' and harshly claiming that they are trying to make themselves into 'Y-list celebs' by taking part in these shows. The writer even implies that these shows are tasteless because we can watch these so-called celebrities 'have nervous breakdowns'.

The writer also objects to the ordinary members of the public who apply to appear on reality television shows. The writer creates the impression that these people are desperate for fame and would do anything – even humiliate themselves – in their quest for this fame, 'these individuals lay themselves open for ridicule and scrutiny by applying for these television shows'.

The writer also insults the audiences of these programmes, 'I suspect the viewers have their phones firmly on redial'. The writer also criticises American reality television shows for their influence on Britain, with shows such as 'the Osbournes' and 'The Anna Nicole Smith Show', 'whoever would have thought that both sides of the Atlantic would have been gripped by the antics of Ozzy Osbourne?' The writer gives us the impression that reality television shows are bad and includes rhetorical questions, 'Should it really be on television?' to make us think about what we are watching.

"Can't take my eyes off Baku ..."

♣ What are the writer's attitudes to Azerbaijan?

STUDENTS' RESPONSES TO THE QUESTION

i

The writer thinks that this is the longest trip made by Welsh fans. He is happy he is going to Azerbaijan. He is looking forward to the football game and he hopes Wales are going to win. He arrives in Azerbaijan and reads the list of dos and don'ts they give him to read on the plane. But it does not put him off going and he is still looking forward to it. The people in Azerbaijan are very friendly and the children even play football with him and his friends. The writer is not very happy because the children beat him at football. He is glad that he doesn't live in Azerbaijan because the city is dirty and filled with smoke.

ii

The writer has mixed feelings about Azerbaijan. He is looking forward to going because he has never been there before and he was taking part in 'the longest European trip ever undertaken by Welsh fans'. He is obviously excited about the football match, but he is also interested in the place and the people.

He uses the trip to do charity work with other Wales fans 'a few Wales fans had the idea that we would do fundraising work for local orphanages in Baku.' He does not boast about the work he is doing. He feels he should try to help the people in Azerbaijan who had suffered 'the recent war with neighbouring Armenia.' Although the writer clearly wants to help the orphanages, his idea of helping seems a bit strange. He brought the children, 'Wales shirts, footballs, complete kits, toys, and signed pictures of Giggsy ...' The children were very grateful and this made the writer feel like he had done something to be proud of.

As he travels through the city, he is moved by the situation of its residents. He feels sorry for them and the reality strikes him, 'this gave us the first real feeling that a lot of Baku residents are really struggling'. He was surprised by the appearance of the city. 'the main part of the city was surprisingly affluent'. But as they carried on he started to feel guilty, 'whole families were living in shells of buildings, huddled round small fires for warmth, and us just there for a football match'. This quote shows how much the experience has changed him. He is genuinely moved by what he has experienced in Azerbaijan.

Thinking Green – Seeing Red

◆ What is the writer's attitude towards conservation?

i

The writer has mixed views about conservation. At the beginning the writer says that it is not enough to recycle at home and also says that we feel guilty for putting the bins out. He gives out a strong message by saying that that's only a small price to pay. It's obvious that he feels strongly about conservation and making the planet cleaner, but it seems that he is not prepared to put the effort in. He seems to think that it is too much effort to put lettuce leaves on the compost heap instead of in the bin. I get the impression that he is angry because he has to sacrifice some essentials, such as driving. He does not want to share a car with the boss or his lover. He also gives me the impression that he thinks that conservation is a bit of a hassle because he says that they've got enough to worry about in the workplace, without having to remember to save electricity or to recycle paper.

ii

In this article the writer is obviously taking a rather cynical view towards conservation policies in the workplace. This is clear from his regular use of sarcasm, 'stray piece of lettuce'. He also makes an appeal for support to the reader, 'made to feel guilty … for doing our jobs!'

His opinion could be considered by some as rather controversial. The writer does therefore clearly justify 'conserving the planet', saying it is 'a good thing and has very obvious benefits'.

This is a very tongue-in-cheek piece, to be taken lightly so as not to cause offence.

As well as using justification, rhetorical questions are used to appeal to the reader, 'And who could disagree that that's only a small price to pay?' There is also a sense of everyday humour that is designed to appeal to readers, especially office workers, who can identify with the humorous problems, 'David Brent-like workmates' and so on. Another way the writer appeals to the reader through humour is in the use of exaggeration.

iii In the article the writer gives mixed views about conservation. Although the writer is clearly in support of saving the planet, he does not think that this should become an obsession and it should not get in the way of the day-to-day running of our lives. He talks about how he agrees with the latest initiative to conserve energy and to be green, but as the title suggests he also sees the problems and gives a more cynical (and humorous) view.

The writer controversially states that we are being 'made to feel guilty' about failing to recycle at work and at home. Although he understands that it is good that we try to conserve the planet and that we would all benefit in the end. He finds it hard to change his habits, 'driven to the point of going through our rubbish'. This indicates that he obviously is feeling the strain of keeping up with good habits and is also ridiculing the extreme to which the government feels we should take conservation to. He thinks it is too much effort to make sure that everything possible that can be recycled has been removed from the bin.

This attitude is maintained when the writer goes on to talk about how these initiatives should be moved from the home to the workplace. He has a very cynical view on this and calls it 'neurotic behaviour'. He talks about the stress that is mounting up as we are expected to recycle everything and how we are made to feel guilty if we dare to forget.

In the article it is suggested that we share cars to reduce the amount of pollution that is released into the atmosphere, but the writer scoffs at this idea too. He immediately points out the downsides and says that this idea would only increase the stress of working every day. The line, 'tempers get frayed' explains how all the colleagues would be in the car together. The writer expresses his opinion about reducing the amount of electricity used. This is about the only thing he agrees with, but even this is tongue-in-cheek. He thinks this would 'save the stress of dealing with computers', but this only because he suggests switching them off! He has resorted to sarcasm to end his message.

Unit 3.2 Comments on the student responses

P Plates!

Answer (i) mentions some good points about the article, but it is short and does not really focus on the question in any depth. This student has merely reported bits of what is said in the article. (Grade: F/E.)

Answer (ii) is much more purposeful and focuses more on the question. The student uses text to support his/her comments. There is obviously some uncertainty about the meaning of 'compulsory', but on the whole this student offers a sensible and accurate response. (Grade: D/C.)

Answer (iii) is a confident response and offers explanations for the quotes selected. It explores how the writer conveys his support for the use of P plates and the impact of this attitude on the reader. It has a clear overview and detailed comments of some quality. (Grade: A/A*.)

Artificial Reality

Answer (i) is quite brief and offers only a limited explanation of the writer's attitude. It is on the right lines but stops short of integrating the details of the text into the statements about sarcasm and the observations about taste. Potentially this is quite a strong answer but there is more to be drawn out of the comments made. (Grade: D/C.)

Answer (ii) offers a comprehensive explanation of the writer's attitude and how this affects the reader. It uses quotes carefully and appropriately, and correctly identifies the writer's patronizing tone. There are some outstanding moments. (Grade: A/A*.)

"Can't take my eyes off Baku ..."

Answer (i) only focuses on the writer's excitement at visiting Azerbaijan for the majority of the response. This student has identified that the writer is looking forward to the game, but doesn't recognize that he is ridiculing the list of dos and don'ts they were given on the plane. At the end of the response, this student mentions that the writer is relieved to be going home, but does not really capture the writer's sense of sympathy for the people who live in Baku. (Grade: E/D.)

Answer (ii) is significantly better, highlighting the writer's range of attitudes towards Azerbaijan, as requested in the question itself. It starts with a reference to mixed feelings and generally maintains the double-edged approach. (Grade: C/B.)

Thinking Green – Seeing Red

Answer (i) does not quite grasp the complexities of the passage, the humour and the sarcasm. Although some good points are made, quotes are not used to support them. (Grade: E/D.)

Answer (ii) is a better response, and immediately identifies that the writer is cynical. There are also some sensible comments about the impact of the passage on the reader. This student will get marks for identifying that the piece is 'tongue-in-cheek', and for describing the techniques used by the writer to convey his opinion. (Grade: C/B.)

Answer (iii) is a strong response because it deals with the passage as a whole and not just individual comments or sentences. This student has recognized that the writer becomes more extreme as the passage continues, using sarcasm as a last resort to convey his message. (Grade: A/A*.)

Unit 3.3 Analysing persuasive techniques

Holiday Fun in Sunny Valley

♣ **How does the brochure try to persuade people to visit Sunny Valley Holiday Camp?**

i

Firstly the brochure claims to appeal to all, 'fun for all ages'. It gives the impression that it can please all, 'even to the most difficult teen'. The article also tries to appeal to difference markets such as single parents. The article boasts of its wide range of activities, from 'Kids' Club Parties' to 'bingo' the aim is for there to be activities to catch everyone's eye. The piece uses words like 'attractive', 'ultimate in luxury' and 'the latest in ...' to create a positive image. This article aims to create a perfect fun-filled image of Sunny Valley in the reader's mind. To add to this the writer uses little details to make the reader think of a wonderful holiday, 'so you can stock up with all the Cornish specialities'. The layout itself, long paragraphs, isn't that eye-catching but the pictures draw the eye into the article. A very friendly image is created '... a holiday should please everyone'.

ii

I believe that the use of persuasive language is effective in the brochure. The brochure includes everyone — people of all ages are referred to. Words such as 'sunny' and 'welcome' are used to create a happy atmosphere at the beginning of the piece. Also words such as 'spacious' and 'attractive' are used to describe the chalets, giving an air of class and quality. 'Sunny Valley' itself is an attractive name because it gives the reader an idea of being in an open and relaxed place, unlike a cramped caravan park.

The writer challenges the reader, tempts the reader to come to 'the ultimate in luxury holiday accommodation' and also for them to take on the go-karting and the rock climbing. The writer knows that parents think that teenagers are hard to please, but the article overcomes this problem by using the 'Teen Club'. Also the 'junior Kids Club' and the 'big Kids Club' are attractive to parents who want a relaxing holiday.

On the other hand, even though Sunny Valley includes everyone and despite good use of persuasive language, it would not be to everyone's taste. In the end it is just another cheap holiday camp, made to sound attractive with appropriate writing techniques. Even Sunny Valley could not beat the value for money offered by holidays to the coast of Spain!

Holiday Fun in Sunny Valley

MEANS OF PERSUASION	COMMENT/EVIDENCE

QUALITIES SUGGESTED	COMMENT/EVIDENCE

WORDS AND PHRASES	COMMENT
'special rates for single parents'	
'the ultimate in luxury holiday accommodation'	
'well-trained staff'	

FEATURE OF PICTURE OR LAYOUT	COMMENT

Young Britons Quizzed Over State of the Planet

♣ **What image of young Britons is presented in this article? How is this image created?**

i

Young Britons are presented in the article as 'passionate about the future of the planet'. This is the opposite of what most people think children understand. This creates a good image of their understanding. This is created by the word 'passionate' which implies that children really care about their planet. Young girls' image in this article is unknowledgeable, as it shows the high percentage of young girls who don't know what happens to their rubbish while the boys know more about the waste system. People tend to think that young children have little or no idea about the environment. This article contradicts that and gives them a good image. The image is created by the writer including the percentages in his article. The article also gives a good impression of the children by showing that 99 per cent put their rubbish in the bin, this would probably shock a lot of people as they believe it's children who create a lot of pollution when it comes to rubbish.

ii

Young Britons are presented in the article as 'passionate' children who worry about the 'future of the planet'. The statistics such as '80 per cent of 10 to 11 year olds say it is very important to look after the environment' creates an image of very knowledgeable children, not that you would normally think about teenagers in that way. It suggests that all the children are worried about the environment by describing schemes and ways that the schools help the environment. The passage gives a better image to boys than girls. A lot of the statistics create an idea that most of the country's girls are quite stupid, 'almost one in five girls think that their dustbins contents "just go away" '. I think that the author creates an image that the British boys are very clever by using a lot of statistics. A very well-educated image of the children shows. The author uses sentences like 'children are all very aware of the importance of trees to the environment'. After this, the writer uses more statistics to prove this. This well-educated image is enforced with an interview with the Environment Minister who says 'we can educate our children about the merit of recycling and the importance of the environment'. This passage creates an image of many knowledgeable young Britons who know a lot about the environment.

iii Young Britons are given a very positive image. They are presented in this article as 'passionate about the future of the planet'. This image is created in the first sentence and a powerful word is used to cement the image. The writer uses favourable statistics to create a positive image of young Britons, e.g. '??% of youngsters put their rubbish in the bin'. Boys also have a very positive light shone upon them – two pieces of the research are used to make the boys sound their best. They are usually seen as less caring for the environment, but this article and the survey suggest that the boys have more knowledge of what and why things happen in the waste business. By using three high-scoring statistics within one sentence, coupled with strong suggestions of the children's awareness of the importance of trees, the article creates the impression that the young Britons quizzed are mini eco-warriors!

The article, in thoroughly focusing on the younger generation, might imply that our society is very aware of the environment because we have taught the children well. The final comment in the article from the government reveals that the Yellow Woods Challenge and similar schemes are a 'fantastic example of how we can educate our children about the merit of recycling and the importance of the environment'. This suggests that Yellow Pages are instrumental in creating an environmentally friendly generation. This comment does as much to promote Yellow Pages as to promote the awareness of the environment in young Britons. Although this mention of the company slightly taints the article, the image created is very strong, effective and positive, one of the young Britons' attitude towards the environment.

The Burning Issue

♣ **How does the reader try to persuade us that deforestation is an urgent problem?**

i In the article 'The Burning Issue' the writer is obviously totally against burning trees, and rainforests being wiped out. The writer tries to get us on his side by telling us all the bad points about his particular subject. In the first paragraph the writer says that people are to blame for the lack of trees in the world because they don't do enough to help. The phrase 'out of sight, out of mind' is used to describe people which means that if there isn't anything about trees in the papers people seem to take less notice of it.

In the second and third paragraphs the writer tells us what will happen if forests do die out. Different species will become extinct, 350 million people that rely on the forests will be homeless or won't have a living, soil erosion, watershed destabilisation and an imbalance in the global climate could happen.

The writer asks a question at the end which is an effective way to get our attention, 'So what can be done?' He then goes on to tell us what could be done to save the forests. After reading the article I feel more aware of what's happening to the forests in the world and I feel we should do more the keep our forests.

ii The writer warns the reader that the deforestation issue is becoming less important to people these days because we tend to focus on the potential threat of war. The writer also produces facts such as 'around 17 million hectares of forest are being destroyed each year'. The large figures have been used to shock the reader. These are frightening statistics to the reader. The writer accuses us the 'population' for being behind this deforestation, this makes the reader feel guilty and really appeals to the reader. The writer also uses pictures to try and persuade the reader, pictures can really appeal to the reader's emotions, it helps us to picture and understand the devastating effects of deforestation.

The writer warns the public that many species may become extinct as a result of the complacent public. This may shock the reader to think that we could be killing off rare living things, plants, animals, birds, etc. The writer also frightens the reader by emphasising that if we don't put a stop to deforestation many undiscovered species will become extinct before we even know about them. This can make the reader upset and make them want to help with the issue. When the writer talks about how 350 million people worldwide rely on the forest for food, shelter and fuel these statistics could really appeal to the reader's emotions and persuade them immensely. The urgency carries through to the end of the article when a solution of sorts to the problem is given. It all sounds a bit too simple to me, but the main thing is that the reader's awareness has been raised to a level of urgency.

At the Heart of the World's Greatest Marathon – FLORA

♠ **How does this article try to convince us that the London Marathon is the world's greatest marathon?**

i

This article tries to persuade you that it is the best marathon by simply saying that it is. The article uses a lot of facts and figures to support this claim and says that millions of people take part each year and raise millions of pounds for charity. The article says that people can run in fancy dress if they want to and this makes the marathon sound like the most fun marathon in the world as well as the greatest. The article also includes lots of comments from famous companies and famous people all saying that it is the greatest marathon in the world and how much fun it is. This is why I think it is the greatest marathon in the world.

ii

The writer goes straight to the point and says, 'The Flora London Marathon is now recognised as the greatest city-centre marathon in the world'. The reason for this is because he makes us think right from the start that this statement is correct. The writer then goes on to tell us that the 'runners and media … organisers of other leading marathons worldwide' also think this. The article does this to convey the idea that everyone thinks this. Then, the writer goes on to tell us about the 30,000+ entrants, 'current and past Olympic and world champions, world record holders, amateur, club and fun runners'. The writer conveys the idea that it is a 'unique and memorable occasion' by saying, 'thousands of participants run to raise money for their favoured charity, many wearing weird, wonderful and often cumbersome fancy-dress outfits'. This also reminds us that this is a charity run.

The writer tells us of how much money the London Marathon raised for charity, 'over £150 million has been raised' since 1981. Eight years is a long time to be the sponsor and the writer tells us how the partnership 'has flourished due to a good fit between sponsor and event'. The writer then tries to persuade us to take part in the marathon, by saying, 'why not take up the challenge and apply for the 2003 event?' He then tries to persuade us further by telling us to think of the long distance as a challenge for ourselves. At the end they give us a list of people giving praise to the marathon, which makes us think that the London marathon is the greatest in the world.

Unit 3.3 Comments on the student responses

Holiday Fun in Sunny Valley

Answer (i) offers only a limited insight into the persuasive techniques used in the brochure. Comments are supported by short quotes from the text, but this student has not really understood how the writer is so persuasive. Sunny Valley is appealing because it offers something for *absolutely* everyone and this is demonstrated in the brochure. (Grade: E/D.)

Answer (ii) is a confident response which recognizes the majority of the techniques used in the brochure to persuade you to visit, even ending with a sceptical comment about British holiday camps! (Grade: B/A.)

Young Britons Quizzed Over State of the Planet

All three responses recognize that young Britons are described as 'passionate about the environment' and all three understand that the children are shown in a positive light. Even answer (i) recognizes that this favourable opinion of young Britons differs from how most people imagine them to be. The better responses in answers (ii) and (iii) not only identify that statistics are used to convey this positive image, but also how they do this and what the statistics mean precisely. Answer (iii) incorporates conservation-type language into the response: 'mini eco-warriors'. This answer presents a far better use of language than that in answer (ii) where the statistics are described as showing that girls are 'stupid'.

Grades: answer (i) – E/D; answer (ii) – C/B; answer (iii) – A/A*.

The Burning Issue

Answer (i) understands the urgency of the de-forestation issue and reiterates the writer's comments about how it is currently being ignored in the press. It makes some good points but does not include significant textual detail to support the comments made. (Grade: C/B.)

Answer (ii), although relatively short, is much more focused and explains in detail the persuasive techniques used by the writer to get the public to think about deforestation. However, there is scope even here for more detailed references to the text. (Grade: B/A.)

At the Heart of the World's Greatest Marathon – Flora

Answer (i) does not really answer the question properly. It merely makes superficial comments about the article and these are not supported by much textual detail. This answer is not focused on the task and does not have much to say. (Grade: F/E.)

Answer (ii) is much more accurate and largely stays focused on the article. Quotations are used to support the comments made and some of the student's reactions are given. This answer covers a great deal of the article and focuses on many different reasons as to why the London marathon is considered the greatest in the world. It also offers reasons why people should be taking part. (Grade: C/B.)

Unit 3.4 Comparing non-fiction and media texts

The Moon Landing (First question)

♠ **Which of these two texts, the report or the article, do you find more interesting – and why?**

STUDENTS' RESPONSES TO THE QUESTION

i The video advert is trying to get you to buy the video. The video shows that the moon landing was a hoax. The advert uses lots of different things to make you buy the video. There are lots of different fonts and the heading is very bold to get your attention and make you read the advert. The advert uses clever words to get you to buy the video, such as 'compelling' which makes the video sound unmissable. The advert uses comments from lots of people who say that the video is good and that the moon landing was a hoax. There are also lots of questions in the advert which make you ask yourself these questions about whether or not the moon landing was real. I think the moon landing was real, so I don't think this advert is very good because I wouldn't want to buy the video.

ii The newspaper article is quite interesting because it makes space travel sound very interesting and exciting. The article describes that space travel has a long history and it makes you want to be a part of that, 'astronauts mark 30th anniversary of moon landing'. There is no mention in the article that there are claims that the moon landing did not take place. It just describes how it did take place and what it felt like for the people who actually walked on the moon.

The advert is much more interesting than the article though. It is really interesting and makes you think really hard about what you think about the men landing on the moon. You start to believe that the moon landing was faked when you read the advert. All of the questions in the advert make you wonder about what happened on the moon and it makes you think that if it isn't a conspiracy and they did land on the moon then why are people claiming that they didn't. This really makes you believe that the moon landing was a conspiracy and it didn't really happen. The advert says that the video is 'supported by detailed analysis and the testimony of experts from various disciplines.' This really makes you think that if professional experts say it's a fake then it must be. It really makes you want to buy the video.

iii The advertisement is more interesting and convincing than the newspaper article, because it makes you question everything you believe about the moon landing. It forces you to ask yourself if the moon landing genuinely happened and if not, how was the footage produced. Whether you believe the moon landings were real or not, the video sparks your curiosity and you would want to buy it because you want to know 'what happened on the moon' – if anything. The newspaper article treats the moon landing as a fact and although Cerman's descriptions of his experiences on the moon are very interesting, the advert is intriguing and you want to read that rather than the article.

There are always lots of stories about the moon landing, but there is not much publicity surrounding the claims that the moon landing is a hoax. The advert is deliberately trying to provoke a response from the reader by using rhetorical questions and carefully selected quotes from 'experts'. However, by reading the quotes more closely they do not actually state that the moon landing was a hoax. 'It's remotely possible' implies that the chances are quite slim that the moon landing was not real. This quote also implies that the moon landing actually took place, but that maybe 'some of the film was spoiled'. So the quotes do not actually support the claim of the advert that the moon landing did not take place. The article does not give much information about actually being on the moon. It reminisces about NASA's previous space missions and speculates about the future of space travel, 'we'll be on our way to Mars by the turn of the century'. But after reading the advert you begin to wonder if they'll fake the footage of that as well.

The Moon Landing (Alternative question)

♣ **Both of these texts are concerned with the American moon landings. In what ways are they similar and in what ways are they different?**

i I prefer the first report because it is a true story about the moon landing. It has a very clear headline which says that the last moon landing was 30 years ago, but the report ends saying it won't be the last. 'Not only will we go to the moon, but we'll be on our way to Mars by the turn of the century.' The other text doesn't believe the Americans ever landed on the moon. In the headline, they ask a question 'What Happened on the Moon?' and they answer the question by saying 'A benchmark which might be invalid. What happened on the Moon? The video will reveal all.' The first report has a picture of an astronaut on the moon and the second has a video to say it doesn't believe that.

ii The similarities between the two texts are that they are both concerned with the American moon landings. The newspaper report uses the 30th anniversary of the last moon landing to remember the Apollo astronauts and missions. The reporter interviews Eugene Cernan who was the last astronaut on the moon and there are lots of quotes and comments by him. Part of the report is about Apollo 13 which could not land on the moon because of a ruptured oxygen tank. The other text seems like a newspaper report, but it is an advert for a video about the moon landings being faked by NASA. It also has quotes, one by an astronaut, and one by Quentin Falk from the Daily Telegraph. So the first text celebrates the moon landings and the second text questions them, even though they both suggest that the Apollo missions had some problems. The second text obviously likes asking questions because it is trying to make people curious enough to buy the video. There are probably more differences in the texts than there are similarities.

iii The two texts relate to each other directly, but they are different types of texts trying to do different things. Bob Thomas' report for the Houston Chronicle is mainly informing the public readers of a celebration event for the anniversary of the moon landings. It is quite funny to think of all the astronauts thinking of famous words to say while they are on the moon. It is not really trying to be controversial, but it does raise the issue of the problems that Apollo had. It is not all celebration – the writer reminds us of 'near-fatal mission' and the 'near-disaster' and 'cancelling' and it says that 'The scientific community was very dissatisfied.'

'What Happened on the Moon?' takes the mystery further. It mentions NASA's 'embarrassment', suggesting there was a cover up about some of the film taken which might have been shot in a TV studio. Basically, it whets your appetite to buy the video with talk of 'conspiracy theories'. In fact, right from the start it sows seeds of doubt about the moon landings with 'The majority of us believe we went to the moon in 1969 ...' Doesn't everyone believe it?! So this text is all about selling a video, rather than reporting the truth.

The Moon Landing

SIMILARITIES (i.e. close comparisons, but not necessarily identical features)

REPORT (*Houston Chronicle*)	ARTICLE/ADVERT (Video)

DIFFERENCES (moving towards contrasts or opposites)

REPORT (*Houston Chronicle*)	ARTICLE/ADVERT (Video)

A Language Study – Water

♣ **Compare the advertisement and the encyclopedia entry.**

i The two pieces about water are from different places. The one is an advertisement and uses descriptive language to make the water sound good so that people will buy it. The second one is from an encyclopedia and it is very factual and boring to read. It is just for people who want to know what water is and all about it. The fonts in the advertisement are very fancy and eye catching, whereas in the encyclopedia entry it is just a normal standard font because it is not really trying to catch anyone's attention. I preferred reading the advertisement but the description of water is a bit unrealistic. But the encyclopedia entry was very realistic.

ii The first piece of text is taken from an advertisement and its aim is to persuade you to buy the product – Brecon Carreg Water. The second text is taken from an encyclopedia and its aim is to inform you about what exactly water is. This shows that the two texts are very different. Because they have different aims this means that their layout, content and words used will all be different. The words used in the advertisement make the water sound wonderful and delicious, but this is very different to the encyclopedia entry, where it says that water has no taste at all! This makes the advertisement sound like it is lying to make you buy the product. The encyclopedia presents facts and it does not contain any lies or does not stretch the truth. It just tells you exactly what water is and what it is like. The advert uses all different fonts to catch your attention and make you interested in the mineral water. The encyclopedia uses an ordinary font because it is just offering information and is not trying to get you to buy the water.

POINTS TO CONSIDER	DETAILS AND/OR COMMENTS	
	ADVERT	ENCYCLOPEDIA
The purpose of each text		
The content of each text		
The image of water in each text		
The choice of language in each text		
The overall presentation of each text		

Teaching (First question)

♠ **Which aspects of these texts do you find effective in influencing your views on teaching?**

i

The first text really puts me off wanting to teach. The school Mick Jagger went to was dangerous and the pupils treated the teachers really badly and disrespected them. This would not at all make me want to be a teacher, especially in that school. The second text makes teaching sound wonderful and something that is fun to do, with all the plays and trips you can go on with your class. It makes teaching sound like something everyone would want to do. In the second text, it does not tell you about naughty children and problems in the classroom, like in the one about Mick Jagger. It only tells you the good bits about teaching, whereas the Mick Jagger text only tells you the bad bits. This is why I think the second text would make me want to be a teacher, but the first text wouldn't make me want to be a teacher at all.

ii

The first text didn't influence me in wanting to teach at all. There was real violence between masters and pupils', people don't want to have violence in their work place. The second text is much more effective and influences your judgement more. Although it is trying to persuade you into teaching it gives facts and most of them are positive. I find the first text much more alarming and the school seems very out of date. The second text is much more friendly and conversational 'you'll be educating and shaping the development of a new generation'. This makes you feel special and fulfils its aim. It also brings in the active side of teaching, which will appeal to a wider range of people, 'hilarious school plays and trips', but it does say that 'It's hard work. Teaching requires the highest level of commitment.', so that might put people off. The first text influences you not to go into teaching, but the second does make me want to teach as most of it draws you in and shows the best of teaching.

iii The first text does very little to influence anyone to be a teacher. Just the opposite, if anyone thought that they would have to put up with all of the violence, they would head straight for a job at Kwiksave. However, Mick Jagger does realise it is different now, so in a way the text is effective in showing how things have changed. In fact, this article does start to be positive ('self-discipline rather than corporal punishment') and describes the exciting new performing arts centre at his school. In the end, Jagger is saying all that violence is a thing of the past. Obviously though it is the second text that influences your views more on teaching. It's a clever recruitment advert really, because it is quite straightforward – not a heavy read – and it targets the reader directly with a highlighted 'you' right at the top of the page. It asks lots of questions at the start and packs the first paragraph with positive vocabulary like 'inspired', 'excited' and 'committed'. Then it gives the headline – a more straightforward question – and proceeds to give you the answers in four high-tech bullet-points, each of them beginning with a really short definitive statement ('It's fun … It's life changing … etc'). It really appeals to anyone who is enthusiastic or it tries to motivate you to believe it's you! It is full of uplifting phrases about making the world a better place – 'helping young people turn their ambitions into reality', 'fulfil their aspirations'. It paints a totally rosy picture – 'hilarious school plays' (NOT!) and 'share in the enthusiasm and excitement of young people'!! It does mention the hard work, but ends by denying it's boring. The last words are smug – 'Boredom is not on the syllabus.'

Teaching (Alternative question)

♠ **The images of teaching presented in these texts are very different. In what ways are they different?**

STUDENTS' RESPONSES TO THE QUESTION

i The first text makes teaching sound violent, but the second text makes teaching sound very exciting and rewarding. It warns you that 'it's hard work' but it also makes teaching sound like fun so it doesn't matter that the work is hard too because you'll have good fun in the job. The bullet points make the article easy to read. This makes the job sound good because there are more good things about it in the text than bad things. This makes you think that maybe you want to be a teacher because it sounds so rewarding.

ii In the first text, the image that is given is of a very strict education. The teachers are very strict and their classes are very disciplined. There is no bond between the teachers and the pupils. The relationships between the teachers and their pupils are very violent. 'There was real violence between masters and pupils'. This is the opposite of the second text, which encourages bonds between the teachers and pupils, and any kind of violence towards the children is not tolerated. The second text talks about the pleasures of teaching, the fulfilment of preparing a child for the rest of their lives. It draws your attention to the main points about teaching, 'it's fulfilling', 'it's life changing', 'it's hard work' and 'it's fun'. The first text does not mention any kind of pleasure that a teacher could have from teaching. In the second text it says as closure to the text, 'boredom is not on the syllabus' while the first text is about how boring school and teaching is.

iii Both of these articles are quite biased in the way their views of teaching are presented. The first text presents a very negative view of teaching, with references to how the pupils used to assault their teachers. Mick Jagger's school days are described as 'something out of a comic book'. This immediately makes you think that if you become a teacher you will have to face cheeky children who will play pranks on you. Mick Jagger says this is exactly how his school days were, 'there were paper darts, pea-shooters, catapults.' The second article makes teaching sound like a complete joy and nothing at all like the way Mick Jagger describes it. This article admits that teaching is 'hard work' but this is something of an understatement when you consider what Mick Jagger's teachers had to put up with.

The second article gives teaching a positive image and does not mention anything about problem children or the abuse that some teachers get in the classroom from their students. Instead it says, 'People forget how much fun working with children and young adults can be'. This is so ironic after reading the article about Mick Jagger. His teachers must have found his class anything but fun and he even admits, 'our class was one of the better ones so I hate to think what the less interested groups were like.' This is a completely different view of teaching compared to the second article. However, Mick Jagger does admit that teaching has changed a lot since he was in school, 'I read in the prospectus that the emphasis is now on self-discipline rather than corporal punishment, which is wonderful'. This implies that today teaching is nothing like it was when he was in school, which is what the second article tries to explain. So overall these two articles are not very different in what they say about teaching today, though in the second text it is idealistic and doesn't mention any discipline problems that still exist.

Unit 3.4 Comments on the student responses

The Moon Landing (First question)

Answer (i) shows a superficial understanding and makes the mistake of focusing on only one of the two texts. There is a very limited use of textual detail and no real demonstration of technical knowledge or the persuasive techniques used. (Grade: F/E.)

Answer (ii) is slightly more developed, with the focus on both texts rather than just one. There is also a promising use of quotation and a limited explanation of the techniques used in both texts. (Grade: D/C.)

Answer (iii) is a developed response showing well thought out ideas and a confident use of quotation. The high levels of analysis shown demonstrate that this student has a good understanding of both texts and the techniques used by the media to attract readers' attention. (Grade: A/A*.)

The Moon Landing (Alternative question]

There is a lot to learn from answer (i). It is evident from the early words that this is not a response to the question asked. There is a very superficial understanding of the texts, borne out by the random selection of details from them. The final comment confirms the lack of focus on the reading. (Grade: F/E.)

Answer (ii) genuinely attempts to answer the question and uses central details of the texts to do so. The student picks out both similarities and differences and attempts to link them. However, it lacks a little cohesion and focus. (Grade: D/C.)

Answer (iii) reveals some close work on language as well as confidence in dealing with the purpose of each text. It is a nicely rounded answer. (Grade: B/A.)

A Language Study – Water

Answer (i) is fairly vague and does not go into much detail in the comparison of these two texts. This student has grasped the different purposes of the texts but the discussion mainly focuses on superficial details such as the font and the layout. (Grade: F/E.)

Answer (ii) is rather better. This student has identified the relationship between the purpose of a text and its design features. This student focuses on the different contents of the two passages – even stating that advertising bends the truth, whereas the encyclopedia uses only facts. (Grade: D/C.)

Teaching (First question)

This is quite a difficult question to focus on because it requires students to create a coherent view from two contrasting texts, related to their own existing views on teaching.

Answer (i) focuses mainly on the first text and Mick Jagger's views on his school days. It describes why this text would not influence readers to go into teaching. It does not, however, clearly explain why the second text *would* make you want to go into teaching. (Grade: E/D.)

Answer (ii) uses the material rather better, but overlooks the potentially negative influence of the first text. It does make the central points about the pros and cons of the second text coherently, and ends with a clear summing up of the effects of both pieces. (Grade: C/B.)

Answer (iii) is very assured, working out intelligently the way the first text works, responding personally to the way that the article develops and changes. The effect of each text is measured, with coverage of the 'recruitment advert' strong on selection of detail. (Grade: A/A*.)

Teaching (Alternative question)

Answer (i) is a very limited response. There seems to be some secure general understanding, but little close reading, especially on the first text. (Grade: F/E.)

Answer (ii) is significantly better because it is more balanced in coverage and more detailed, though rather lacking in depth. (Grade: D/C.)

Answer (iii) is a thoughtful response. This student has covered both texts quite thoroughly and has made a real effort to compare the images of teaching. The clarity of summary of images (negative/positive) allows the answer to proceed with purpose. (Grade: B/A.)

Extension work on non-fiction and media reading

Using the texts – extending the questions

The pairs of longer texts in Unit 3.4 of the *Students' Book* are comparable in length with non-fiction and media texts used in Section A of Paper 2 in the English exam.

Below are examples of questions that could be compiled by teachers for fuller work on non-fiction and media texts. They cover the range of four questions and are based on the two 'Teaching' texts.

Foundation Tier questions

1. List ten unpleasant things that Mick Jagger remembers from his school days.

2. According to Mick Jagger, how has his school changed since he was there?

3. How does the advertisement try to interest readers in a career in teaching?

   In your answer, comment on:
   ♣ what the advertisement says about teaching
   ♣ the choice of words and sentences
   ♣ the layout of the advertisement.

4. The images of teaching presented in these texts are very different. In what ways are they different? (This question also appears in *The Students' Book*.)

Higher Tier questions

1. According to Mick Jagger, what was wrong with education forty years ago?

2. What is Mick Jagger's attitude now to his old school?

3. How does the advertisement try to interest readers in a career in teaching? (Consider what the advertisement says, and how it says it.)

4. Which aspects of these texts do you find effective in influencing your views on teaching? (This question also appears in *The Students' Book*.)

NOTE In 'live' exams, the texts used in Paper 2 Section A of the Foundation Tier will always be different from those used in the Higher Tier. The nature of the reading texts themselves will form part of the differentiation between the tiers in addition to the extent of structure and guidance offered and the degree of emphasis on higher level skills.

Section 4: Transactional and discursive writing

Introduction

Section B of English Paper 2 tests the skills of writing by setting two transactional and/or discursive writing tasks, one of them based on the reading material of Section A, followed by another free-standing task. Student responses are judged against two broad sets of criteria:

- *content and form* – accounting for the greater part of the weighting
- *sentence structure, punctuation and spelling* – the lesser part of the weighting but intrinsic to the overall success of any piece of writing.

These criteria are covered in the fourth section of the *Students' Book* within three units:

4.1 Writing to *argue, persuade, advise* – transactional writing

4.2 Writing to *analyse, review, comment* – discursive writing

4.3 Technical accuracy in transactional and discursive writing

There is considerable common ground between transactional writing and discursive writing. Transactional and discursive writing tasks both require students to have a strong sense of audience (often very specific) and purpose (the impetus and direction of a written response). A sense of format is also needed, particularly in transactional writing, where the layout of letters, leaflets and reports is quite an important visual support for a student's engagement with a task. In discursive writing, traditionally regarded as 'the essay' but here represented by articles and reviews, there is again no scope for leisurely digression – a journalistic 'edge' (or, at least, an aptitude for clear thinking) is a key quality of successful responses.

Expectations of students' knowledge of topics and issues covered by these 'closed writing' examination tasks are not unreasonable. A transactional or discursive task linked to Section A (media/non-fiction texts) obviously provides specific material that is there to be 'used' by students in Section B, but it should be explored rather than copied, adapted rather than lifted, highlighted for selection rather than downloaded in bulk. Personal opinion is not only valued, it is a pre-requisite of argumentative and persuasive writing.

Similarly, the free-standing task (i.e. the task not connected to the Section A reading material) will feature a rather general topic (borne of the restrictions of the 'common assignment') and the expectations of 'expertise' will be realistic. The *content and form* section of the marking criteria is couched in terms of arguments and ideas, and not knowledge and understanding.

Technical accuracy ('sentence structure, punctuation and spelling') is judged alongside 'content and organization' in the assessment of writing. Within reason, errors are tolerated, particularly where a student is ambitious in style and word use. Careless errors are costly, however.

Two answers are given for each of the tasks in this section. Comments on the answers are included at the end of each unit. The answers were written by GCSE students in roughly the 30 minutes that would be allocated to a single writing task in the exam. Teachers might wish to follow this principle when using the *Students' Book* – students discuss and plan to 'a state of readiness', then answer the question 'against the clock'.

Mark scheme for transactional writing

Transactional pieces should be assessed by making best-fit judgements across and within the broad grade bands. In 'best-fit' judgements, weaknesses in some areas are compensated by strengths in others. For practical purposes, students could be advised to consider *content and organization* first, then to confirm or refine judgements by considering *sentence structure, punctuation and spelling.*

Content and organization	Sentence structure, punctuation and spelling
G/F ♣ Basic awareness of purpose and format ♣ Some awareness of reader and audience ♣ Some relevant content ♣ Simple sequencing, some coherence ♣ Paragraphs may be used for some order ♣ Some attempt to adapt style ♣ Limited range of vocabulary	**G/F** ♣ Mostly simple or compound sentences ♣ Conjunctions such as 'and' or 'so' ♣ Punctuation attempted where appropriate ♣ Simple spellings usually accurate ♣ Uneven control of verb tense and agreement
E/D ♣ Awareness of purpose and format ♣ Awareness of reader and audience ♣ Reasons support opinions/ideas ♣ Sequencing of ideas coherent ♣ Paragraphs logically ordered/sequenced ♣ Clear attempt to adapt style ♣ Some range of vocabulary, with some effect	**E/D** ♣ Varied sentences, compound and complex used ♣ Some subordination for clarity ♣ Some control of range of punctuation ♣ Simple polysyllabic spellings, usually accurate ♣ Generally secure control of tense and agreement
C/B ♣ Clear understanding of purpose and audience ♣ Clear awareness of reader/audience ♣ Appropriate reasons support opinions/ideas ♣ Ideas shaped in coherent arguments ♣ Paragraphs for conscious structure ♣ Range of vocabulary, creating effect	**C/B** ♣ Range of structures, varied sentence length/focus ♣ Effective simple, compound, complex sentences ♣ Effective, accurate range of punctuation ♣ Most spelling correct, including irregular words ♣ Secure control of tense and agreement
A/A* ♣ Sophisticated understanding of task ♣ Sustained awareness of reader/audience ♣ Well-judged, detailed, pertinent content ♣ Convincingly developed arguments ♣ Paragraphs effectively varied and controlled ♣ Sophisticated use of stylistic devices ♣ Wide range of appropriate vocabulary	**A/A*** ♣ Effective variation of sentence structures ♣ Sophisticated, effective use of range of sentences ♣ Accurate punctuation for deliberate effects ♣ Correct spelling, including complex irregular words ♣ Confident, purposeful tense changes

Unit 4.1 Writing to argue, persuade, advise

Transactional writing – letters

♣ **Write a letter to your MP. You may argue for or against the use of animals in experiments.**

i

Dear Mr. John MP.

I have one question, why? What is the real point in animal experimenting? What are the reasons for doing it? If humans are so intelligent why do you need to choose the poor animals fates? Can't they do that?

What actually gives you the right to test on these animals as research shows that seven out of ten animals die in your "experiments" as you so call them, when can we justify being deliberately cruel to these Animals?

O.K. so they may be needed to see if there's a cure for peoples diseases, but can't you take some blood from your self and then test, no!!! because you need to test on these animals.

The Top scientists have shown that cancer has tripled via Animal testing how do you Justify that?

Yours sincerely,

ii

(addresses and date supplied)

Dear Sir/Madam,

I am writing in response to an article I read in your newspaper dated Tuesday, 12 November. After reading the article I felt I had to write and inform you on some facts that I think you will find very interesting.

I have lived on a farm for many years and everyday I am involved in feeding and general care of the many livestock and domestic animals. Therefore I have a wide understanding of their needs. I would like to convey my point of view on the topics of animal testing, cruelty and hunting whilst making it clear to you I have grown up with animals and have a deep respect and love for them.

Firstly, I want to inform you about the motives and reasons for hunting. This is a tradition that has developed and been important for several hundred years. Constantly on our farm we have expensive livestock killed and watch our prospects for profit and for improvement of our standard of living and farm completely ruined as calves, sheep and chickens lie dead, killed and tortured by hungry foxes. If we did not hunt and control the fox population we would be in desperate trouble – as would thousands of farmers around the country. Do you not think it is hard enough for us to face a crisis such as BSE and watch our months of hard work destroyed in a storm without foxes destroying our hopes as well?

Although I am in support of organisations such as the WWF, I feel that they are such huge organisations that their views are taken as standard and correct and the opinions of people who work with and care for animals everyday are dismissed and simply unheard. There is even outrage by the public about the farmers milking their cows too much. I would very much like to know how the city folk who have never had the experience of working on a farm have come to this conclusion — and how government ministers can come to conclusions without any experience or much knowledge themselves. Therefore, I am sure you can appreciate and understand the barriers we have to constantly work against and push down in order to make a successful living.

Also, several years ago, my grandmother died of cancer, followed shortly after by my aunt. This, as you can imagine, caused widespread grief in our family. There is no cure for their disease which plagued them for so long and caused so much pain. So why is the testing on animals to find cures met with so much resentment? I am sure if people had personal experience of death they would certainly feel the same way. Of course, testing on synthetic cells or tissues would be a better and more humane way forward but at the moment we have to ask ourselves why the death of several mice and rats should be seen as so significant when many humans are dying from presently incurable diseases and causing grief and upset to so many.

I only wish for you to accept another point of view and perhaps reconsider your opinions with this new information.

Yours faithfully,

♣ **A newspaper has recently printed an article arguing that movie stars are paid too much money. Write a letter to the newspaper giving your views on this issue.**

STUDENTS'
RESPONSES TO THE
QUESTION

i

(addresses and date supplied)

Dear Mr Jones,

In my opinion I think that movie stars get way too much money for what they do, they should donate more money to charity and stop keeping it for themselves. Compared to nurses they get paid on average 1 million pounds every film which works out to be about £500, 000 per hour and their not even saving peoples lives where nurses are and their on minimum wage. This can't be right.

Yes I think that actors a very talented but still their not

worth the amount of money they get payed. It not just the movie stars that's getting all this money all the celebrities are, the money that they have should be used in a more usefull way like the NHS and making places better for sick people and more things like that.

This is what I think of all this money getting wasted on celebrities but I don't think it's going to make much difference.

Yours sincerely,

(addresses and date supplied)

Dear Sir/Madam,

I am writing in reply to the letter published last week, regarding the amount of money paid to movie stars and other celebrities. While I agree with your correspondent's views that these people are paid ridiculous amounts of money considering how many needy people there are in the world, I feel a few points need to be clarified.

Firstly, the people who pay celebrities are different to those who can help the poor and homeless. The sports, music and film industries are huge, multi-million pound businesses and those involved are paid the going rate. Much of the money generated is through advertising and sales and this money is acquired fairly. As long as someone is willing to pay the money for a latest album or dvd, the industry will charge it. Of course, I doubt many of these celebrities deserve the money but it is still acquired legitimately.

Homelessness and poverty are social problems and as such, must be dealt with by society as a whole. Pointing the finger at celebrities, overpaid as they are, doesn't solve the problem. No single person can be blamed, these problems can arise because of all of us. From overpaid 'stars' who avoid paying taxes to each of us who don't put money in charity boxes, we can all be blamed in equal measure.

To the author of last week's letter, I agree that these large salaries aren't deserved. However, instead of begrudging them the money, why not focus on helping those who need help? By setting an example, your friends, family and workmates will soon follow suit and maybe one day we'll all be earning obscene, superstar salaries.

Yours faithfully,

♣ **Write a letter to your head teacher or principal with your recommendations for improving the appearance of the school or college.**

i

(own address and date supplied)

Dear Sir,

I am currently attending your school in Year 11. My purpose for this letter is to suggest some ways of improving the appearance of the school.

I have had many different ideas, however here are the more eye-catching ideas for the school. Firstly I believe that the school front gates need to be repainted, because the old paint has worn out and they have a considerable amount of rust on them.

Secondly, a colourful welcoming sign would improve the school's importance. The schools formality would increase: appearance wise.

Thirdly the schools front wall should be widened and some plant pots should be placed on top. This would improve the natural appearance of the school.

Finally, and the most important is to paint the entire school a colourful colour or even colours. This would dramatically improve the appearance and brighten up the school.

Yours sincerely,

ii

Dear Sir,

I am writing to you today on behalf of the college. I am a student that attends Any College and will be writing about the appearance of the school and what I recommend that you could do about it. As a pupil of the college I think that it is write that I could have my say.

I will start talking about the food canteen, I do not think personally that there is enough choice on the menu especially for vegetarians, seeing as I am one myself it seems that I have the same meal about three times a week. Now if there was more choice I think would be eating the meal I have less than three times, so I recommend that you have more choice for vegetarians to choose from. As for the other food you sell in the canteen they do seem to have more choice, I hope that you can at least think about my comment rather than just saying No.

Nevertheless the girls toilets in the college have never got toilet roll in, I could probably say the same for the boy toilets aswell. I should think you can understand because it probably get on your nerves aswell when you walk into the toilet and don't have no toilet roll to use.

Dispite this I am not atall happy with the grafetti that has been spred around the college it looks a real mess especially when we have people to look around. I hope that you will think about my comments.

Yours sincerely,

♣ **The government has decided to crack down on anti-social behaviour, which might mean anything from dropping chewing gum on the pavement to drunken behaviour in public. Write a letter to your local newspaper discussing anti-social behaviour in your area and how it might be tackled.**

i

(addresses and date supplied)

Dear Sir/Madam,

I am writing on behalf of the safety of the public in the Any Town area.

I read an article that you published last month about anti-social behaviour and it shocked me to read the statistics of the amount of fights caused by drunken behaviour.

My class came up with a few ways in which to crack down on this kind of behaviour. You could increase the amount of security in lager pubs then they will be able to stop fights before they get out of hand.

A second point could be that if the fights or bad behaviour does spill onto the streets closer contact with the police could be an issue.

Please take these points into consideration.

Yours faithfully,

ii

(addresses and date supplied)

Dear Sir/Madam

I am writing to you to discuss how to crack down on anti-social behaviour in my hometown. I am concerned with the amount of teenagers hannging around on street corners with nothing to do but shout out rude or threating comments. There is also though's who graffity and litter our streets. Alot of elderly people are also very scared to go out at night because of these young youths. Although we only have three pubs in the area one of them stay's open all day everyday which is another concern as some of the youths hang around outside asking people to get them drink or cigaretts this the same outside the local shops. I am not saying that the pub should close during the day as the owners would lose alot of business with the tourists that come to the village. The long beach gets littred alot and has no beach patrol to make sure the rubbish goes into the bins provided. This then meens that animals get harmed and many even die. As a teenager myself, I feel that a youth club should be set up as well as other activities. I also feel a skate park would make a difference and would then get teenagers off street corners. If the government are willing to put any preposells forward I would be greatful if they could come to the village.

Yours faithfully,

Transactional writing – leaflets

♣ **Write a leaflet for elderly people offering advice about safety in the home.**

SAFETY IN THE HOME

THE KITCHEN

The kitchen is one of the dangourest rooms in the household.

The dangor in the kitchen is:

- Knifes being left out
- Cooker left on (can cause a fire)
- Ioner being left on where children can get to it

BATHROOM

The bathroom can also be a dangores place because:

- The bath can over flow
- Electric radio can fall into the bath
- All electric applias must be kept away from the sink and bath

GARAGE

The garage has many dangoures things there. There are:

- Tools left out
- Poisenes liquids
- Garden tools
- Sharp blades
- Cables

Picture of skull and crossbones

- Poisen

ii *TAKE CARE, BE SAFE*

Just because you're getting on a bit, doesn't mean you need your own minder. BUT – do be careful around the home. Be safe from others – and be safe from yourself.

Most people think their home is the safest place to be. You want to feel safe both in the daytime and at night. Well, get yourself a security chain fitted and keep your door locked to strangers at all times. If the gasman comes to the door, ask to see his identity card.

Keep in touch with people. Use the phone. Let your family know how you are and don't be afraid to ask for help with DIY. We don't want you falling off step-ladders or severing an artery when your screwdriver slips.

Is your memory not what it used to be? Then find some way of reminding yourself of certain dangers like leaving the gas on. Use stickers to jog your memory – CHECK THE GAS! LOCK THE DOOR!

OUTSIDE DANGERS

Gardening is an excellent way of keeping active when you are getting on in years. Just remember to do a little on a regular basis. Don't overdo it and seize up! Get the right tools and a lawnmower that you can control. Don't leave tools lying about where you might trip over them.

Watch yourself underfoot. Keep an eye on the weather forecast and, if it's frosty and icy, resist the temptation to stroll to the shop along a slippy pavement. Wait a while until it thaws.

REMEMBER – we don't want to lose you! Have a long and happy retirement.

♦ **Write a leaflet warning younger pupils about the dangers of fireworks.**

i

DANGERS OF FIREWORKS

THE LAW

You will be arrested if you buy or sell fireworks. You must keep away from them because they are mostly elleegal for you. You should ring the police and tell them if you see anyone bying or selling fireworks when they should'nt be.

CHILDREN

Children should never be alloud to go near fireworks, except may be sparkellers because they are pretty and fairly safe as long as the adults are watching and they don't mind they're children playing with sparkellers and speling their name and having fun.

BE SAFE

Only let adults near fireworks. Do not touch them. Do not go back to a firework even if it has not gone off. Always make sure there is a bucket of water near buy incase you're fireworks start a fire.

Photograph of a person with lots of burns from fireworks

DANGER!!!
XXX

ii

DANGERS OF FIREWORKS

Everyone knows fireworks are dangerous. So how can we all be safe around them and still have a happy and exciting bonfire night? Hundreds of youngsters get injured every Bonfire Night — make sure you are not one of them.

Just follow these simple guidelines and you will stay safe.

FIREWORKS AND THE LAW

It is illegal for anyone under the age of 18 to purchase fireworks. This also means that it is illegal for anyone to sell them. If you know of anyone who has purchased fireworks illegally or is selling them to people that they shouldn't then you should contact your local police immediately. Throwing fireworks at people or pushing them through people's letterboxes are both classed as criminal offences and you will be arrested by the police if you are caught doing these things.

FIREWORKS DISPLAYS

Although firework displays in your own garden are very popular, they are also potentially very dangerous. Always make sure that the fireworks are stored in a cool, dark, dry place far away from any possible sources of sparks or flames. Never hold a lit firework (unless it is a sparkler) and never light a firework indoors. Make sure you stand well back at a firework display and never return to a firework once it has been lit, even if it has not gone off. The best and safest answer is to attend a public firework display.

PUBLIC DISPLAYS

Every area will have a fireworks display organised for the locals. These events are usually free and much more exiting than little garden displays because there are more people and larger displays. There is also usually a large bonfire and hot-dogs and jacket potatoes on sale for the spectators. These displays are usually carefully planned and well organised, taking all of the worry out of fireworks night. It is always better and safer to attend a public display than to have your own.

BE SENSIBLE

The important rule is to be sensible with fireworks. So long as you are using your common sense, there is no reason why you cannot enjoy fireworks night safely.

Transactional writing – reports

♦ **Write a report for your local council outlining ways in which the area surrounding your home could be improved.**

i

Report to the Village Council

Introduction

The area surrounding my village is mostly fields, there are not many activities for the young children. There is only one park and no other areas for young children to play. Apart from fields.

The Procedure

When visiting my local village I handed out questionnaires to 10 adults and 10 children aged 8 to 16 years old. The questions were based on "how to improve the area surrounding my local village" In each questionnaire there were 20 questions. Most of the childrens answers replyed saying "we want more places to play, hangout and more activities, e.g. swimming, netball, youth club, etc. Also they said they wanted another park with more bins to keep the park clean and safe, unlike it is now. The adults didn't really want to change the surroundings as they liked the scenery, but some said they could do with some local supermarkets as it would be easier than having to travell to the next town.

The questionnaire results showed that both adults and children agreed and said that there could be a lot more done to keep the countryside clean.

Recommendations

I recommend than an activity centre is built for the children and young adults. Shops could be built for parents who are unable to drive or who have young children. The scenery could be made more intresting, which would attract tourists.

Conclusion

In my conclusion the area surrounding this village is plain and lifeless and could be made more intresting by building a swimming pool, more shops, etc. This would make the area feel more welcoming to people passing by. Also the area is untidy and dangerous to children and animals so a recycling area could be built.

ii PROPOSAL FOR IMPROVEMENTS TO _____ VILLAGE AND SURROUNDING AREAS

To: Chairperson of Council and Council Members
From: Representatives of Local Interest Groups

This report follows concerns raised in the local press about the state of _____ and the lack of facilities for people of certain age groups. An open public meeting was organised and several concerned groups of people attended.

<u>Problems Identified</u>
- Lack of facilities for young people: There are no indoor facilities currently available in the evening and at weekends for young people of school age. There have been complaints by residents in parts of the village about teenagers congregating menacingly on street corners.
- Villagers complained at the lack of recycling facilities in the area. Currently, it is necessary to drive 15 miles to the nearest superstore to offload bottles, boxes, newspapers etc.
- Bus service: Villagers demanded more reliable and more frequent buses and they also wanted a shelter to be built in the centre of the village. They suggested a mini-bus service.
- Safety on the roads: Parents are very worried about the safety of younger children. Cars are speeding through the village, so traffic calming measures are badly needed, as well as an extra zebra crossing and a lollipop lady.

<u>Recommendations</u>
- A larger range of activities of village hall activities for teenagers and younger children.
- The building of a fitness and leisure centre.
- A recycling area
- A non-alcoholic pub for teenagers
- Traffic calming measures
- Re-opening of the local mini-market

<u>Conclusion</u>
The community enjoys living in _____, especially during the summer. However, there is a need for the council to do everything it can to improve the quality of life for the people practical ways.

♦ **Write a report to the head of your school or college from the student committee, suggesting how to organize the annual Open Day. Your report should argue how the school or college needs to appear attractive to prospective students and parents, and also how money can be raised for the benefit of student facilities.**

i

SCHOOL OPEN DAY

Report to the Headmaster from the School Committee

For a school open day the school needs to be clean and tidy and all the litter must be in bins and not on the floor or on the playing field. The school should have a big clean up to make it look better. The paint work should be redone and the fences should be mended. This will make parents think that it is a good school because it is so neat and tidy.

The school should have big colourful displays everywhere showing all of the best work done by the students. This will impress the parents and make them think that the children who go here are very clever. It will also show parents the kind of fun school work that their children would be doing if they came to this school.

The school should also have a senior member of staff to meet the parents on the open day, prefrably the Head, because this will make the school seem very friendly and interested in its students.

Finally, the school should consider advertising on the radio, or local television, or in the newspapers. This would attract lots of attention from parents and they would want to come and see the school to see just how good it really is.

Conclusion
There is lots that can be done to attract new students:
- Make the school nice and tidy looking
- Repaint all of the school's doors and windows so they look like new
- Have the Head ready to meet the parents of new students
- Advertise the open day as much as possible.

SCHOOL OPEN DAY

Introduction

The annual school open day is approaching and there are many things that can be done to make the school appealing to prospective students. By asking the students and parents what they are looking for in a school I will be able to assess how to attract new students to the school. In addition to this I will also ask for ideas about how to raise money for the school.

Attracting New Students

I questioned the students who had recently moved to this school to find out what attracted them to come here. From the questionnaire I found that most students thought the school had a friendly atmosphere and is neat and tidy. However, the students said it would look more attractive if there was a trophy cabinet. They also said that they would like to see a "Hall of Fame" with pictures of the school's most successful students. Finally they suggested having displays of students' work throughout the corridors to show the kind of work that will be done in school.

Raising Money

I questioned parents and students about how to raise money for improving students' facilities. Some of the ideas were quite ordinary, such as having sponsored events, such as a fun run or a sponsored silence. However, the students have taken part in these kinds of events before and are not really interested in doing them again. The more interesting ideas involved holding a fashion show, where parents pay to see clothes designed and modelled by their children, and a play or show which parents pay to watch. Finally an auction was suggested, where local companies donate products and services and people bid for them.

Recommendations

- To attract new students to the school I suggest the school takes out an advertisement in a local paper that reaches the school's catchment area. The advertisement should outline all of the benefits of the school.
- The school should organise a trophy cabinet for displaying awards.
- The school should put departmental displays up around the school.
- The school should also put up a "Hall of Fame" showing how successful the students who have attended the school are.
- For raising money the school should hold an auction. Local businesses could then become involved by donating services or products to be bid for. An auction would bring in the most money because it is an unusual event.

Conclusion

It would be easy for the school to make a few minor adjustments to the appearance and presentation of each building to attract new students. It would also be easy for the school to raise money to improve student facilities by holding an auction. However, it would take careful planning and preparation to ensure that the auction was a success.

Transactional writing – speeches

♣ **Write a speech for the general public in favour of the argument that the age limit for driving should be raised to 21.**

i

The age limit should be raised because there are too many people who just pass their driving test and the year after they are allowed to drink, which is very dangerus because they would be to drunk to remember not to drive home and then they will lose their license.

If the age limit for driving was raised, it would stop boy racers driving other cars off the road by scaring everbody. Boys are immature and they always show off, they risk there own lifes and others. It doesn't matter if they kill themselves, but they end up killing other people as well, in other cars and pedestrains.

It would help young people to save their money also, because they always waste it on cars, petrol and things. Not everbody can afford to buy cars so it would be fairer for everone not to have a car untill everbody was 21.

ii

I am speaking in favour of the driving age to be raised to 21. This would be an unpopular decision among young people, but it would be a very good idea for the wider public. Basically, there are two reasons — safety and finance.

Firstly, safety. Government figures show that accidents involving young drivers are out of all proportion to the number of young drivers on the road. Young drivers and passengers are regularly involved in tragedies, when all four (or more) youngsters die instantly in a head-on crash at speed. How often have we read of someone passing their test and driving wrecklessly immediately after? They need protecting from themselves. Speed is the temptation — the opportunity to show off to your mates or to impress a new girlfriend, without thinking for a minute of what damage you can do to yourself and others, including those innocent people in other cars or walking along the street. Raising the driving age limit to 21 would remove peer-group pressure, because if your friend has a car, then another friend, then you want one too.

This brings me on to the second point, money. How can every young person hope to afford to buy a car when they are still at school, college or university or they are unemployed? Surely parents can't be expected to pay for an extra car? Many of the cars that young people drive are bangers and they are not roadworthy — another reason why so many accidents take place. It would surely be better for the law to be changed so that young people can actually save or spend their money on other safer things.

♣ **Write a speech for the general public arguing that professional boxing should be banned.**

i

I was recently reading my local newspaper when I came across an article which deeply shocked me as I believe it must have shocked many people across the country. It was, of course, an article about the horrific consequences of boxing. The fight that it was refering to was between Spencer Oliver and Sergei Devakov. The descriptions were vivid and the picture which was with the article stunned me completley. The amount of pain and despiration on Oliver's face was unbelievable as he fell to his knees begging for mercy. As much as I hear people standing up for this bloodthirsty sport, saying that it's the young men's choice, if they want to compete or not, if you had seen the look on this man's face and the descriptions of his state you would never believe that this was what he wanted. In my opinion, young men aren't warned enough about the dangers of this sport and they are coched at a very young age to believe that it is a macho, manly thing to do. Well I believe it's wrong. I also came across a factsheet which actually said that boxing taught the need for law and order and helped the teaching of self-discipline and respect. How could something which is condoning beating each other half to death possibly teach the need for law and order?

As we know there have been cases of brain damage and even death from fights for example Michael Watson, who now has permanent brain damage from a supposedly safe fight. I'm asking, how many more men are going to have to die or suffer serious injuries until people learn?

ii *How many people would like to be brutally beaten while millions watched, cheered and clapped? Every time a man walks into a boxing ring the slightest blow may cause permanent damage. Why do people box? To make money! Boxing is one of the most highly paid but also controversial sports in the world.*

Boxing originated as street fighting. It was unsupervised and the rules were unclear. People used to take bets, money changed hands on the winners and losers. There were no doctors standing ready to treat probable injuries and mostly the fighters were too poor to seek medical attention even if they needed it desperately. This is because boxing has always been the way some poverty-stricken people living in underprivileged areas have supported themselves and their families.

Some people claim that because of all the 'so called' improvements, legalised professional boxing is a good thing and much better than the slaughter that used to take place in the streets before its introduction.

But have you ever thought about what is happening every time a punch lands to the head? When a blow lands and the brain rotates and hits against the inside of the skull? Well, this damages brain cells that cannot be replaced.

Many boxers have developed diseases because of punches made to their brain. Muhammad Ali won the world heavy weight championship many times in his day. But after retiring developed a disease called 'Parkinson's Disease'. This is a neurological problem due to a loss of brain cell, which may I repeat cannot be replaced.

When all is said and done no matter what, boxing remains the only sport undertaken by human beings whose main aim is to seriously damage your opponent. The fact is the only way to win the fight is to inflict serious and therefore permanent injury.

♠ **Write a speech to be made to fellow students either for or against women going back to work once they have had a baby.**

Today I am going to talk to you about women going back to work after having a baby. I am for women going back to work. Many people have different views on this topic.

I think women should go back to work for numerable reasons. Women spend time with their babies after giving berth, they bond. Once the baby has settled down, the mother should go back to work. Some mothers believe that they should stay home with their children untill their old enough to go to Nursery. Women who decide to go back to work enrolle their children into a Nursery, to be around other children their age. It's in the childs best interest to leave them with other babies therefore the mother could go back to work and earn money, which would benefit the child.

The mother probably hasn't been out socialising in quite a while, due to the baby. Which isn't a bad thing, because the parents chose to have a baby. When the mother goes back to work she will be socialising and meeting knew people once again. Some men expect their wifes to stay home with their little child. Whilst the father goes out to work and has no problem socialising. If both parents would go back to work, they'd have much more money to spend on their child. The child wouldn't miss out much as he or she would be with other children their age. They'd be with a qualified Nanny for about five to six hours depending on the hours the parents work.

All in All Mothers should go back to work to earn more money, and to socialise with other people. Whilst their babies are playing with other children safely.

ii *Hello ladies and gentlemen. Today I am going to argue the right whether or not mothers should return back to work once having a baby.*

When a working woman decides to have a child she would normally leave work for a year or so to have and look after the baby. The amount of time that the mother has off work depends on the job and the boss.

In my opinion women should be able to return back to work and carry on as they did before. I think that the only reason why a mother shouldn't go back to work is if she doesn't want to go back to work and the only reason why she has to go back, is because of financial problems with keeping the child. If a mother has financial problems and wishes to stay home and look after the child the mother should be entitaled to have money off the social services.

I think that job swoping when the mother goes out to work and the father stayes in to look after the child is a good idea because the mum can go out and theres somewhere safe for the child to stay.

When a single mother wishes to go back to work she has no where to leave the child. The child has to be left with a carer or Nersary, this may caus the child to feel unwanted.

If the mother is unhappy staying in with the child she would get depressed and take it out on the child, I think that it is much better for the mother to get out and enjoy being with the child when she come home from work.

Unit 4.1 Comments on the student responses

Letter to MP – Animal experiments

Answer (i) is very clearly on task, but it is typical of many casual responses that invite obvious criticism. The layout features of a formal letter have been largely ignored and the substance of the letter is not very thoughtful. There is no real context or introduction to the letter and, although there is some undoubted rhetorical strength in the argument and some sense of organization through paragraphs, the overall impression is one of sketchiness, not least through the growing number of surface errors. (Grade: F/E.)

Answer (ii) is a huge achievement, especially when one considers the time constraints. It dwells too much on hunting and farming issues but still easily reaches the A/A* band of criteria.

Letter to newspaper – Overpaid stars

Answer (i) is properly organized and offers a clear, coherent viewpoint. Though the piece is undeveloped, it is not far short of a satisfactory length, but the argument posed can easily be countered, particularly when figures are paraded that are probably guessed and are calculated on the length of a film rather than the duration of its production. A little more all-round attention is needed in a piece like this. (Grade: E/D.)

Answer (ii) takes up a stance of defending the rights of celebrities and does so with considerable control and worldly awareness. The argument is mature and sophisticated, the logic impeccable and the tone and expression excellent. A/A* qualities in every respect.

Letter to headteacher/principal – Improving appearance of school/college

Neither of the two examples here is outstanding, but they both show reasonable understanding of the task and the letter genre. They have clear ideas and quite good organization. Arguably, the first letter is better focused on the visual appearance of the college and has a more formal style, while the second letter develops its ideas rather more and makes some strong personal points. Both fit the E/D section of the mark scheme and there may well be some dispute as to which is the stronger response. Needless to say, both could be improved with proof-reading.

Letter to newspaper – Anti-social behaviour

Each of these responses has positive features, but also some obvious shortcomings. They have the correct layout and positioning for a formal letter. Answer (i), though brief, has in its favour the fact that it is orderly and that it sets out to make points clearly. It also ends politely, if bluntly. However, the student appears to have no appetite at all for exploring the issues raised. (Grade: F/E.)

Answer (ii) does genuinely attempt to discuss the issue and manages to raise a range of points, with constructive suggestions offered. However, it lacks the organization of paragraphs, its expression leans towards spoken English and it is prone to surface errors. (Grade: E/D.)

Leaflet – Safety in the home

Both of these answers have design and layout features of leaflets that reflect well on what is possible for students to achieve in an exam. The boxes in answer (i) are not necessary for a successful leaflet written under exam conditions. Many candidates, however, would see them as part of their engagement so they could be seen as a positive feature, along with the quickly sketched outline of a picture. More pertinently, there are sub-headings and 'bulleted' information, both features contributing to the linguistic merit, albeit on a simple level. Nevertheless, this is a straightforward response, very unsophisticated, without a main message and with no direct communication to the intended audience: the elderly. (Grade: F/E.)

In contrast, answer (ii) is vigilant in addressing the correct audience directly with a succession of imperatives, clear statements and the odd question. There is some (perhaps unintended) humour which can be gratefully appreciated in the patronizing tone! The texts of such leaflets do not have to be hugely ambitious – clarity and coherence are far more important, though the occasional turn-of-phrase does mark this out as high calibre. (Grade: A/A*.)

Leaflet – Dangers of fireworks

Answer (i) tries forceful rather than gentle persuasion as a means of addressing the (young) audience, but does sustain the tone consistently. The intended picture would add to the uncompromising approach. The whole piece lacks the ring of truth, however, and the strident commands in reality become hard to bear. Punctuation is carefully applied on the whole, but spelling is quite frail. (Grade: E/D.)

Answer (ii) is quite skilful and much more likely to engage readers young and old than the first. There may be some doubt about the precise target audience in the way language is used discursively on occasions, but the points made are constructive and thoughtful. (Grade: B/A.)

Report – Local improvements

Both of these reports are comfortably on task, but there are one or two features of the first response particularly that invite comment. Answer (i) is dominated by the writer's personal view and generally lapses into a loose informal style. The ploy of using 'Procedure' in such a report is not recommended – by and large the report should deal with the substantive issue, in this case the village – rather than the methodology. Generally, this first report is on the right lines with its layout and ideas, but the lack of formal precision weakens it. (Grade: D/C.)

Answer (ii) is in all respects stronger. Aspects of the format, including the heading, give the report an air of authority. Particular touches of language support this as well and generally it is a clear overview of the situation taking in a range of viewpoints. The style slips marginally in places and the recommendations are slightly undeveloped (presented as a blunt list), but overall this is a fairly impressive examination response. (Grade: A/A*.)

Report – School or college open day

This is an interesting pair of responses because both have obvious qualities and weaknesses. Answer (i) is not particularly stylish, but it is quite well focused on clear points of recommendation. The expression attempts to be formal, with the writer successful in giving a representative view rather than personal opinion. (Grade: D/C.)

Answer (ii) is a full response and makes many points with precision. It uses layout features purposefully and displays use of appropriate vocabulary. Even though it is written in the first person, the student displays a secure command of standard formal English. The commitment to the task is considerable and the writing coherent. (Grade: A/A*.)

Speech – For raising the driving age limit to 21

This is not an easy task because the raising of the driving age limit to 21 would be deeply unpopular with young people, almost to the point of mutiny! Answer (i) is not a strong response. As well as some very obvious errors, it displays poor logic and reasoning from beginning to end. There are some ideas worth considering but they are disconnected and there is little sense of it being a speech, either formal or informal. (Grade: F/E.)

In contrast, answer (ii) is well argued and skilfully organized. It is clearly presented with features of formal speech, but not in a pedantic way. Expression is almost entirely accurate (though 'wrecklessly' is probably an unintended pun). Points are made directly and developed enough to present a credible case. This answer sounds as if it could be spoken persuasively, with stresses, pauses and a good variety of sentence length. (Grade: A/A*.)

Speech – For the banning of professional boxing

Answer (i) is informal, but no less of a speech than a more conscious piece of rhetoric because there is cohesive, persuasive control of a fiercely argued position, with complex structures and several strong connectives. It does have the spontaneity of a spoken reply in ongoing debate. Less convincing, but still valid, is the rather contrived use of accompanying reading material. Errors on the surface are irritating, but they do not greatly weaken the performance. (Grade: C/B.)

Answer (ii) is rather more authoritative, a more measured performance, including a controlled and powerful opening paragraph. This student appears to bring historical understanding to the topic, which is a bonus in a closed writing response. Technically very accurate. (Grade: A/A*.)

Speech – For or against working mothers

Neither of the responses on working mothers is outstanding but the second one emerges as rather stronger than the first. They are of similar length and are both prone to errors but the second response is, sentence by sentence, more coherent. Answer (i), though clear enough, stutters even in the first paragraph. As the piece develops, the lack of fluency becomes more pronounced, with comma splicing, incorrect sentence demarcation and indifferent logic spoiling some good, if rather naïve, ideas. (Grade: E/D.)

Answer (ii) is reasonably well-considered, with a clear strain of responsible and mature values. The argument cautiously moves forward, looking sensibly at a range of issues. The frequency of errors is slightly troubling. (Grade: D/C.)

Mark scheme for discursive writing

Discursive writing pieces should be assessed by making best-fit judgements across and within the broad grade bands. In 'best-fit' judgements, weaknesses in some areas are compensated by strengths in others. For practical purposes, students could be advised to consider *content and organization* first, then to confirm or refine judgements by considering *sentence structure, punctuation and spelling*.

Content and organization	Sentence structure, punctuation and spelling
G/F ♣ Basic awareness of purpose and format ♣ Some awareness of reader/audience ♣ Relevant comment; basic analysis ♣ Simple sequencing; some coherence ♣ Paragraphs may be used for some order ♣ Limited attempt to adapt style ♣ Limited range of vocabulary	**G/F** ♣ Mostly simple or compound sentences ♣ Conjunctions such as 'and' or 'so' ♣ Punctuation attempted where appropriate ♣ Simple spellings usually accurate ♣ Uneven control of verb tense and agreement
E/D ♣ Awareness of purpose and format ♣ Awareness of reader/audience ♣ Sense of purpose in analysis/comments ♣ Coherent sequencing of details/comments ♣ Paragraphs logically ordered and sequenced ♣ Clear attempt to adapt style ♣ Some range and selection of vocabulary	**E/D** ♣ Varied sentences, compound and complex used ♣ Some subordination for clarity ♣ Some control of range of punctuation ♣ Simple polysyllabic spellings, usually accurate ♣ Generally secure control of tense and agreement
C/B ♣ Clear understanding of purpose/format ♣ Clear awareness of purpose/audience ♣ Clear sense of purpose in analysis ♣ Analysis/comment shaped for viewpoint ♣ Ideas shaped into coherent arguments ♣ Paragraphs used consciously for structure ♣ Style adapted to purpose/audience ♣ Effective range of vocabulary	**C/B** ♣ Range of structures, varied sentence length/focus ♣ Effective simple, compound, complex sentences ♣ Effective, accurate range of punctuation ♣ Most spelling correct, including irregular words ♣ Secure control of tense and agreement
A/A* ♣ Sophisticated understanding of task ♣ Sustained awareness of reader/audience ♣ Well-judged, detailed, pertinent analysis/comment ♣ Convincingly developed analysis/comment ♣ Effectively structured analysis/comment ♣ Paragraphs effectively varied and controlled ♣ Sophisticated use of stylistic devices ♣ Wide range of appropriate, ambitious vocabulary	**A/A*** ♣ Effective variation of sentence structures ♣ Sophisticated, effective use of range of sentences ♣ Accurate punctuation for deliberate effects ♣ Correct spelling, including complex irregular words ♣ Confident, purposeful tense changes

Unit 4.2 Writing to analyse, review, comment

Discursive writing – articles

♣ **Write an article for the school magazine discussing the options for students once they have completed their GCSEs.**

STUDENTS' RESPONSES TO THE QUESTION

i

Year 11, your GCSEs are coming up, how you do in these exams will help determine what sort of life you will lead after you leave school. The way I see it you have three options at the end of your GCSEs.

One, you could go to college or university and study a subject which relates to the occupation you will take up later in life. To get into college you will need some qualifications but you are able to sit your GCSEs in college if you did not get any in school. To get into university depending on the course you are going to take you will need A Levels.

Two, you could stay on in school and study four subjects which you need to go on to university or get a job.

Three, you could get a job as soon as you leave school. Without any qualifications though you probably won't get a very good job.

So what I'm saying is get some qualifications to get the job you want.

ii

It's coming around to that time of year again, when Year 11 do their GCSE exams and you are probably wondering what you are going to do after them, do you stay on in school, go to college or go out to work and earn a bit of money.

Well hopefully this article will help you to decide. Many pupils will decide to stay in school and do their A Levels in familiar suroundings, which is probably the safest option, because you know the teachers, know people there and also you know the layout of the school.

Many pupils also go to college, its a new experience and can be tough as you don't know many people, you don't know any of the teachers and also you don't know the layout and sometimes a new place can seem like a maze to navigate around. But if you want to specialise your education more, this is probly the best for you.

If you don't fancy carrying on your education then there is not many other options for you than to go to work. It can seem the easy way out but can also be the toughest. With no A levels and not many job oppertunities, it could go wrong and you could get stuck in a dead end job that leaves you depressed and angry.

In my opinnion, staying in school is the best option, but it is completely up to you of course.

♣ **Write an article for the school magazine discussing the ways that the school can be more environmentally friendly.**

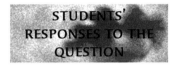

STUDENTS'
RESPONSES TO THE
QUESTION

As you will know the world is constantly being polluted by cars and factories. America has a large role in this pollution, which is not helped by the fact that they don't really have that much interest in making it better or trying to cut down on their pollution. This leads to much more serious affects on the earth, the biggest one is the hole in the ozone layer which will lead to an increase in the risks of sun cancer. We are the new generation and this will affect us, there for it is important that we try and help from a young age.

I know there is not much we can do about the pollution from the factories but if we pull together there are some small things we can do to help. You could join the 'green peace' they will send you all kind of information about how to be more environmentally friendly. Our school could do more too like recycling paper. There is so much paper that just get Chucked in the bin when it could be recycled. We could also place alluminium can recycling bins around the school and pupils could bring in alluminium cans from home and they could be recycled, we could have competitions and the School house with the most cans would win.

Just by picking rubbish up you can help make our school a nicer, cleaner, happier place to be. If you see some sweet rappers on the floor then pick it up and put it in one of the bins provided around the school. This is quit a small school with allot of pupils, which is an advantage.

Being environmentally friendly can be fun it's not just work. Next time you think about chucking rubbish on the floor stop and put it on a bin and make your school and your world a tidier place.

ii TURNING SCHOOLS GREEN

Being environmentally friendly doesn't have to be boring. There are many initiatives that schools can introduce to make the school a greener place to be. Starting with … making the school a greener place. Planting shrubs and flowers in available spots around the school will attract insects and other small animals to the school. This could be a joint initiative between the Geography and Biology departments in the school, which would develop interest in wildlife in students of all ages in the school.

In addition to this, simply placing rubbish into bins is a good way of improving the appearance of the school. The school should ensure that there are plenty of bins around the school for the students to use. However many there are, there can never be enough, because students tend to make a lot of rubbish!

The school's Home Economics department could develop a display for the school showing how our rubbish could be recycled or reused. This would mean that all year groups in school could contribute to the display, may be even incorporating rubbish and waste in the display to show how it can all be used. This is a simple way of informing everyone in the school about how to make their working environment a more pleasant place to be in.

Finally, competitions could be organised — year groups against year groups, classes against classes, team houses against team houses, even staff against students. The competitions could be who can recycle the most rubbish in a school term, who can collect the most rubbish from around school or even suggestions from the staff and students about practical ways of improving the school environment. It is worth remembering though that with all of these suggestions the most practical ways of making the environment greener begin with you. It is only when people realise the responsibility they have to make the world a better place, that the world will actually begin changing.

♣ **Write an article for a travel magazine that describes the attractions of a place of your choice.**

STUDENTS'
RESPONSES TO THE
QUESTION

i *LIVE IN LANZAROTE*

Two years ago I visited the island of Lanzarote, one of the Canary Islands. It is off the coast to the west of Africa. The volcanic islands are full of tourism. A pleasant four hour flight and your there. Lanzarote is known by locals as the 'windy island' due to its fairly windy weather. It is the smallest of the other three islands; Tenerife, Gran Canaria and Fuetuventura. As you fly in to the island you notice how little cloud and how much sunny weather they have. Although Lanzarote is semi-desert, there are more and more palms being planted there, and are well watered. Sun rises at about 7, and then sets at 7, almost everyday althrough the year. It is like summer here in Britain all year through. Most of the people at Lanzarote are employed due to tourism. Shops and restaurants and hotel workers are very common. The island is owned by Spain and there is a lot of Spanish culture and food. The restaurant we went to everyday had great Magerita pizzas. The beaches vary from pebbly and stoney to silk and sandy beaches. All the holiday locations are no more than a five minute drive to the nearest beach. Costa Teguisa is the capital of Lanzarote and the town at which we stayed at. The Airport is a ten minute drive from Costa Teguisa. The Resort we were accomodated at Los Zocos, caters self-catering, half board and full board. If self catering, fear not, there is a supermarket and restaurant, just outside the hotel. There are many shops and British pubs in the centre of Costa Teguisa. Buffet restaurants are also quite common.

ii CAERPHILLY – SO MUCH MORE THAN CHEESE

Whenever anyone asks me where I live and I say 'Caerphilly' they always reply, 'Where the cheese comes from?' So, I'm here to set the record straight. Caerphilly is so much more than just cheese. That's not to say that the cheese isn't very good – it is. But there's more to see and do in Caerphilly than eat cheese all day. So enough about the cheese. Here's what else Caerphilly has to offer.

Caerphilly is located about ten miles from both Cardiff, the country's capital, and Newport. This makes it a popular area of residence for business people who work in the city centre, but cannot afford city centre house prices. This also means that in Caerphilly, you are only a short drive away from a wide variety of shops, enough to satisfy the needs of any shopaholic.

Caerphilly's most striking landmark is an enormous medieval castle, which sits proudly overlooking the town centre. The castle is the largest in Europe but its famous because of its leaning tower. The tower lies at an almost impossible angle and leans precariously towards the moat that surrounds the castle walls. There are many rumours about how the tower got to be leaning. One rumour is that the tower was struck by a cannon ball, but the walls were built so well they could not be destroyed. The real, and less romantic, reason is subsidence, but the locals tend to ignore this and continue to blame a cannonball. Whatever the reason, the castle remains one of the most beautiful sights in Wales.

♠ **Write an article for a women's magazine discussing what life is like for teenagers in the 21st century.**

i

Teenagers in the 21st century have a good time. There are lots to do, like going to the cinema and night clubs and things. There is also good fun in school because we can all get a education and get some good grades. We have lots of things to do like Geography, History, Buisnes Studies, Compters and Engerlish. We can do any job we want so long as we got the qalificasions to do it. Teenagers are quite happy in the 21st century. We got Gamcube and Play Station to play on when we get bored and we can go on the internet if we want to talk to people. We can go skateboading and go shopping for any stuff we want on the web. Teenagers don't have much stress, even though they all say that they get stressed. We don't have a lot to do that makes us stressed. We just hang about and have fun. Teenagers play lots of sports, like tennis, football, rugby and anything you can think of. Girls can do self defence and boys can do martial arts. Girls can even play games like rugby and football if they want to. It is very good in the 21st century.

ii

Life in the 21st century

Most people think that teenagers have a pretty easy time. Although it is true that life is much easier in the 21st century that ever was, life is still tough when you're a teenager. Things that seem like tiny upsets to most of the rest of the world signify the end of the world for teenagers. And believe me, the end of the world seems close virtually every day. From the traumas of spots and bad hair days to the dramas associated with not having a date to the school prom, teenage life is one long hard struggle.

The hardest thing about teenage life though is the fact that we teenagers have virtually no control over the things we say and do. Teenagers spend most of their time just trying to fit in, this takes up the majority of our energy, so we then need to spend time chilling out. This usually involves, surfing the net, hanging out with friends in chatrooms and generally doing anything in our power to avoid doing school work. It's not that schoolwork is any harder in the 21st century, it's just that it seems so boring compared to all of the other activities available to us. It's great doing your homework on a computer, provided you can drop all the other distractions!

21st century teenagers are as relieved as anyone to know that the teenage years don't even last a decade. Although 21st century adults may argue against this, claiming that they last well into their thirties. Some things never change.

Discursive writing – reviews

♣ **Write a review for a topical magazine targeted at young people – EITHER *a review that focuses on one item (for example, a film or a TV programme)* OR a review that looks back over the previous year in some area of interest to you (for example, music, sport, fashion).**

i

'Save the Last Dance'

Save the Last Dance is a film about a girl persuing her dream to become a dancer. Unfortunately her luck changes when on the day of her audition her mum doesn't turn up to support her. Sarah is upset and doesn't understand why her mum would want her to upset her by not turning up. After tripping up and falling in the audition a police officer turns up to speak to her. He then tells her that while her mum was driving to the audition she was involved in a very serious car crash and was killed. Sarah therefore has to move in with her father. She won't dance anymore as it hurts her too much when she thinks of her mum. But when she goes to her new school she meets new friends and falls for Derek. He then persuades her too dance again suddenly her dream doesn't seem such a lifetime away. This film is mainly about music, although it does have scenes of violence. I thought that maybe the film was aimed at mainly twelve or above as there is a lot of violence and some scenes of a sexual nature. I enjoyed the film because it gave the perspective of a dancer living in the 21st century. The film was set in Los Angeles, in this present day. Although the film was about dance there was a lot of romance so I would call this a romantic film. Sarah is the main character of the film; she seems so naive at the start, when she first moves in with her dad. But once she starts making friends you can clearly see that she is strong. At the end of the film they finally accept her as a white girl living in a black community. Derek is Sarah's best friends brother and she first met him in an English class. He is very intelligent and wants to be a doctor when he gets older. But his best friend sells drugs for a living and is on the wrong side of the law, what Derek doesn't realise until the end of the film is that fighting doesn't solve anything and causes trouble in the long run. I would highly recommend anyone who is interested in dance to buy this film.

ii

'The Subtle Knife'

After reading the first novel of Philip Pullman's 'His Dark Materials' trilogy, I was eager to read the long awaited second 'The Subtle Knife', which is set to be as fulfilling as its procceder.

'His Dark Materials' is an epic tale, which moves between different universes. In the Subtle Knife we follow a determined twelve-year-old boy called Will, who is looking for his explorer father, while on the run from the police. While on his mission, he comes across a different world, the Citazze world, a strange and unsettling place, apparently containing no adults. But Will soon finds out the truth about the adults disappearance, their souls have been eaten by the deadly Spectures.

While trying to discover what the Spectures are, Will finds a strange and savage little girl called Lyra. Like Will, she has a mission which she intends to carry out at all costs.

With Lyra searching for her gyptian friend Roger who disappeared from her world, (Told in the first novel of the trilogy Northern Lights) and Will trying to locate his father, they are delayed when, the mysterious Torri degli Angeli uncovers Citazze's most important secret. An object which people from many worlds would kill to possess. Will's journey becomes much more difficult and dangerous, when the Subtle Knife chooses Will to become its new bearer.

This is an exciting and adventurous novel, which I recommend to anyone of any gender to read. Although in some areas the story may become a bit complex for children of a young age, older children and adults can still marvel at Pullmans different ideas and outstanding originality. This book is everything but what you would expect, full of magic and mystery, armoured bears and witches, it is quite remarkable how a paperback can hold so much thrilling suspense and danger. Pullmans marvellous plot and strange characters and remarkable settings make this by far one of the best books I have read this year, (with Northern Lights) and is now on my book shelve, rubbing covers with the likes of C. S. Lewis and JRR Tolkien.

♣ **Write a review for a topical magazine targeted at young people – EITHER a review that focuses on one item (for example, a film or a TV programme) OR *a review that looks back over the previous year in some area of interest to you (for example, music, sport, fashion).***

STUDENTS'
RESPONSES TO THE
QUESTION

i

KARATE

Karate is a sport, it is also a form of self defence. The best thing about karate in my point of view is the fighting and being able to have a fight and not being expelled or excluded like you would in school. Karate is used in many parts of the world, especially America. There are many types of karate styles such as wadoro, which means way of peace. This is the style I'm doing at the moment. This style is used for street fighting. As you progress in karate you get a higher range of belts, which means going from white to 8th black. The range of belts are white, red tag, black tag, yellow, orange, green, purple, brown, brown stripe, brown tag., black, 2nd black, 3rd black, 4th black, 5th black, 6th black, 7th black, 8th black. Between white and purple you have to wait three months between each grading but when its from 1st brown to brown tag its six months between each grading and then for 1st black its 1 year, 2nd black 2, 3rd black 3 years and etc. There are also range of competitions that take place throughout the year. In my club we fight against Pembroke dock and Coventry we also go to a special competitions when all the karate fighters in Wales gather in Cardiff and we fight. In age groups of course and in size that is important to. There are also a lot of injuries testicular cancer has also got worse because people are not using the right gear. I think everybody should do some form of self-defence because it keeps you fit and healthy. It also keeps you fit and healthy mentally so if someone hits you, you get more confident in what you do and the way you react to things and people.

ii Music

Last year saw the rise and fall of many singers and bands worldwide. The most famous career path of all is that of Hear'Say who shot to stardom after winning the infamous television series 'Popstars'. However, their lives were not just full of number one hits and pockets full of money, shortly after their career had began Kim Marsh announced that she was leaving the band and many newspapers blamed the countless arguments between Kim and former band mate Myleen Klass, which the band later denied. Shortly after Kim's split, Johnny, fiancé of ex-Steps member Lisa, replaced her. Hear'Say then changed their image and attempted to bring out a new single to boost their falling sales, nevertheless their single failed to reach the top ten and the band announced their split in 2002, after just 18 months in the limelight.

Following the 'Popstars' series a new band formed, other than Hear'Say, Liberty X, which was made of the five hopefuls who failed to make the band. Although being regarded as 'flopstars' Liberty X went from strength to strength producing numerous top ten hits. Hear'Say was not the only band to split in 2002, they were joined by groups such as Steps, Five and All Saints as they all announced their failed careers. However, 2002 did not only bring bad news to the pop industry, many new 'Pop Idols' such as Will Young, Gareth Gates and Darius who gained fame after appearing on the hit television show 'Pop Idol'. After 'Pop Idol' came the follow up, 'Popstars: The Rivals' where a male and female band were chosen and then had to battle it out for Christmas number one.

Cerys Matthews, lead singer of Welsh band Catatonia, announced her addiction to alcohol in the early months of 2002. Many people were becoming increasingly worried about the number of stars turning alcoholic or becoming addicted to gambling because it was setting a bad example on the younger generation. However, the main worry was raised when the increase of violence was used in R and B and Garage acts as many people were killed at one of the So Sold Crew concerts.

In conclusion, I think that many bands and singers today are in the industry for the money and glamorous lifestyles. Female singers in particular tend to have the Barbie doll image with their extra slim figures which make supermodels look plump. This puts an enormous amount of pressure on their fans that wish to look like their idols.

Unit 4.2 Comments on the student responses

GCSE options – article

Answer (i) is written in a very conversational style, as though the writer is actually talking to you rather than writing. This creates a good effect in a school magazine because the advice offered seems friendlier than if it was written in a more formal style. However, the article is short and does not explore well the options available for students. (Grade: E/D.)

Answer (ii) attempts to offer wider explanation and is generally successful, despite occasional spelling, punctuation and grammatical errors. There is some attempt to extend comments on each option, but the piece remains fairly limited in its discursiveness – offering advice but not probing beyond the general into more detailed areas. (Grade: D/C.)

Environmentally friendly – article

Answer (i) is fairly well focused but there are numerous spelling, punctuation and grammatical errors that detract from the content of this article. There is no title, which would provide a clue to the reader about the contents and would give the piece more purpose. Sentence control is by no means precise, though there is every attempt to be informal and engaging which is appropriate for a school magazine. The basic errors, however, add to the loose expression to weaken the effect of the piece. (Grade: D/C.)

Answer (ii) is a more developed response, with specific focus on two or three possible strategies that have been explained in detail. It offers mature and developed solutions for improving the school environment, and the quality of expression is raised accordingly. It is more comfortable in discussion than answer (i). (Grade: B/A.)

Attractions – article

Answer (i) gives a broad description of Lanzarote. It describes the location and geographical features but does not really focus on the attractions of the island. It lacks a real sense of purpose. There is a limited attempt to describe the facilities available, and this is often awkward. Spelling, punctuation and grammatical errors are intrusive. (Grade: D/C.)

Answer (ii) is a bright, well developed response. Although it is quite a short answer, it focuses well on the attractions of Caerphilly. There is an engaging humour in the opening and beyond, in keeping with the needs of a travel magazine article. (Grade: A/A*.)

21st century – article

Answer (i) contains many spelling and grammatical errors. This student does not seem completely confident with the subject matter and has packed too much information into too few sentences, though the writing is very positive and appreciative. This piece is rather short and although the focus is clearly on answering the question, the style is awkward and no attempt has been made to write specifically for readers of a women's magazine. (Grade: E/D.)

Answer (ii) is a more humorous and relaxed description of teenage life. Occasionally though the comments could be applied to almost any teenager from the last five decades and they do not focus specifically on teenagers in the 21st century. However, this is a well-written and confident piece, which shows awareness of the audience. (Grade: B/A.)

One item – review

Answer (i) offers a detailed, if occasionally confusing, description of the film. It makes what is probably a fairly simple plot sound far more complex than it possibly is. There is a limited attempt to offer opinions on the film, but there is no real awareness of the audience. The student doesn't make much attempt to make this article interesting for the reader – there is only one long paragraph and the sentences are all fairly similar in structure. (Grade: D/C.)

Answer (ii) is a very mature response, despite occasional spelling errors. There is an awareness of audience with less emphasis on retelling the plot and more effort in explaining who this book is suitable for. The piece has a complex, ambitious style with relatively few problems of accuracy. (Grade: A/A*.)

Previous year – review

Although answer (i) is interesting and informative, it does not attempt to answer the question. Rather than describe the events in Karate over the past year, this is more like a beginner's guide to Karate. There is no mention of any of the competitions that happened in the previous year. The article is also quite confusing, with no clear paragraphs. It just seems to be an off-loading of information rather than a genuine attempt at responding to the task. (Grade: E/D.)

Answer (ii) is a very good and well-focused piece. This summary of pop music over the last year is informative and the student even uses occasional sarcasm and humour to convey opinions about the events. There is a real effort to appeal to the reader and to make the piece interesting, with a pleasing blend of 'expert' knowledge and authentic journalese. (Grade: A/A*.)

Extension work on transactional and discursive writing

Linking reading with writing – exploring techniques

Below are two impressive responses by GCSE students to transactional writing tasks. The questions that follow them are 'borrowed' from Section A of Paper 2 to reinforce the link between reading and writing on this paper.

   This is an analytical exercise that could be carried out in class on any successful pieces of exam or coursework writing.

Text 1: A magazine article for American readers

Back to Blighty

There's nothing new under the sun; and it may seem that there's nothing new in Britain, nothing not available in America – and it's not even under the sun.

   If there is one area where Britain can compete with America, it's history. Interested in archaeology? Mad about the Middle Ages? Britain contains some of the most beautiful and well-preserved architecture of ancient civilisations – and unlike Greece or Rome or Egypt, we speak the same language. If you'd like to see where your ancestors got on the Mayflower, it's in Britain, along with many of the ports where families and young people embarked on a ship taking them to the New World.

   Another thing Britain has a lot of is Brits – in their natural habitat! Cut-glass accents or common as muck can be found within an hour's drive. Britain, compared to America, is small but she packs in an awful lot in the space she has. Major cities boast stadiums, museums, theatres, libraries and a lot of shopping.

   London, the capital, in particular has a lot to offer. The West End which rivals Broadway, the Thames (subject of many poems), the Queen – or at least her famous residence, Buckingham Palace, and the Crown Jewels and Tower of London (complete with ghosts), the respected shops such as Harrods or Fortnum and Masons, old-fashioned double-decker buses ... and the chance to see it all from the new London Eye.

   But Britain isn't all towns and cities and smog: there's also beautiful countryside and attractive coastal areas, though bathing is not recommended. The strictly-animal disease of foot and mouth is swiftly clearing. Your limbs will be safe, and rambling in the well-known beauty spots such as the Lake District or more secluded but no less picturesque areas is resuming its popularity. The more adventurous may want to try mountains. Both Wales and Scotland boast famous peaks well suited to the casual or more dedicated mountaineer.

   Britain is no America ... but then, America is certainly no Britain. Try them both!

For discussion or written response:

1. According to the article, why should Americans visit Britain?

2. What image of Britain is presented in this article?

3. How does the leaflet (on the following pages) persuade you to visit Salisbury? (Think about what is said and how it is said.)

4. Both the article and the leaflet try to attract tourists. Which do you find more effective, and why? Consider:
   ♣ purpose and audience
   ♣ content
   ♣ writers' choice of words and the effect they have on you
   ♣ picture, headlines and layout.

Text 2: A tourist guide to Salisbury

ENJOYMENT FOR ALL AGES!

Come and visit the historic and beautiful town of Salisbury. Home to the world renowned Salisbury Cathedral, you can wander the streets and marvel at the medieval architecture.

Set in the rolling Wiltshire hills there is so much to do!

WHAT TO SEE!

Here in beautiful Salisbury, you can take a tour of the town, marvelling at the ancient buildings.

Why not laze on the fresh plains by the river on a hazy day?

Or, for the more adventurous among you, you could even take a flight from the local airfield. Go by small plane, helicopter or even microlite from prices as cheap as £25!

WHERE TO EAT!

There is a wide selection of eateries in the area — and whether you want to devour the food in the pubs or taste the delicacies of the brasseries and fresh bakeries, there is something for everyone.

We recommend the Café Parisian for those of you who are cultured at heart.

Or perhaps the aptly named 'Salisbury Starlight'. By day taste the traditional Wiltshire foods surrounded by memorabilia from the past centuries, and by night experience the dancing, darts and quizzes to enter the local spirit.

WHAT TO DO

For the more mature:

Wander through the cobbled streets, taste the delicacies, purchase gifts or clothes from the wide range of shops we have on offer or simply soak up the atmosphere. You can even take a ride on a horse and cart. Take excursions to experience the pleasure of the stunning landscape and relax in the Cathedral gardens and experience one of the many concerts performed there.

For the young at heart:

The huge selection of trendy shops will entice even the most reluctant of you, whilst there are a number of cheap but good quality eateries to choose from during the day. By night, Salisbury metamorphoses into a young person's haven. Sample the night life, which local people travel miles to experience. Whether you fancy a cocktail bar, a chilled night in a pub or a full-on clubbing experience, Salisbury is the place to be.

For the kids:

There are toyshops galore situated in Salisbury centre, and kids clubs let you escape the clutches of your parents and experience the thrills of the town. You can go karting on the race track, ride the hills on ponies and feast on a huge selection of fast food.

Whatever you choose, you're guaranteed a great time.

So why not give us a ring? We can send you more leaflets with information on the wide range of hotels we have — from medieval themed to a simple bed and breakfast, there is something for everyone.

Pick up the phone now and dial 00000 000000

Salisbury — so what are you waiting for?

Section 5: English literature

Introduction

The English Literature examination requires students to respond to texts and explore their language, structure, form and meaning. Students are also required to relate texts to their social, cultural and historical contexts and literary traditions. These skills are covered in the fifth and final section of the *Students' Book* within five units:

5.1 Responding to extracts
5.2 Discursive essay questions
5.3 Empathy questions
5.4 Poetry appreciation
5.5 Anthology comparison tasks

These units focus on different types of question that are asked in the examination, concentrating on the key features of the questions while recognizing that, in practice, the question will vary from text to text.

The tasks set in Section 5 of the *Students' Book* are generic. They cover aspects of questions that are common to different parts of the English Literature examinations. There is no attempt to cover the specific details of study of each of the prose and drama set texts. Students are encouraged in several of the Section 5 units to search for points of focus as part of their study, in recognition of the need for successful literature candidates to be independent thinkers.

The sample answers in the following pages are therefore not taken directly from the tasks in the *Students' Book*, but are authentic classroom responses to past paper questions. The coverage of the prose and drama set texts within these sample answers is to a large extent random. Comments on the responses are included at the end of each unit.

For Unit 5.1, there are four examples of responses to set text extracts: two from the prose section of the examination and two from the drama section. Emphasis in the commentaries is on skills displayed, rather than knowledge of the text, so it is hoped that the answers can be useful to students whatever texts they are studying. For Units 5.2 and 5.3, there is a similar balance of prose and drama sample answers, the intention being to focus on some of the distinctions between those two genres – again, detailed knowledge of the specific texts is not essential for students to gain some value from evaluating these responses.

For Unit 5.4 responses are provided for each of the four 'unseen' poems included in the *Students' Book*. In addition, two sample responses to poems from Specimen Papers are provided. For Unit 5.5, there is an example of a prose comparison and a poetry comparison, to represent the distinctive requirements of the Specification B examination.

It should be noted that most of the answers in this section are taken from Higher Tier tasks. This reflects the fact that Higher Tier questions and responses are more likely to display close analysis of language, something that the strongest of Foundation Tier candidates also need to show.

Mark scheme

English Literature exam responses should be assessed by making best-fit judgements across and within the broad grade bands. In 'best-fit' judgements, weaknesses in some areas are compensated by strengths in others. The criteria for Specification A exam answers are those in the left-hand column, while certain Specification B exam answers (see Unit 5.5) are, in addition, judged against the criteria in the right-hand column.

NOTE When writing English Literature answers, students should remember that their 'quality of written communication' is part of the overall assessment of their work.

	1. **Knowledge and interpretation of text** 2. **Exploring language, structure and form** 3. **Conveying response**	**Making comparisons** (Specification B exam only)
G	♠ Narrative with some misreading ♠ No exploration expected ♠ Simple expression of opinion with little textual support	♠ Simple, unfocused expression of preferences
F	♠ Some understanding of main features, including characters and themes. Generalized reference to relevant aspects ♠ May make generalized comments about stylistic effects ♠ Response conveyed in appropriate ways. Simple opinion about text, character, situation. Empathy simply expressed	♠ Straightforward connections between texts made. Selection of some obvious features of similarity and difference
E	♠ Narration with varying degrees of clarity and economy. Selection of relevant material ♠ Recognition of, and simple commenting on, particular features of style ♠ Addresses task and uses text to support views	♠ Beginning to develop simpler points of comparison
D	♠ More detailed reference to text – quoting, 'echoing' or paraphrasing as necessary. Awareness of sub-text. Some discussion of characters/relationships. Still reliant on narrative mode ♠ Beginning to see how different aspects of style combine to create effects, e.g. changes in mood and atmosphere ♠ Opinions related to question and conveyed with some clarity	♠ Comparison and some evaluation of (e.g.) subject, character and impact of text
C	♠ Detailed reference to text. Some probing of sub-text ♠ Extended discussion of characters/relationships. Awareness of some of the cultural and social contexts of texts ♠ Some understanding of how meanings and ideas are conveyed through language, structure and form ♠ Points aptly supported by reference to text. Clear and structured response ♠ Able to sustain character's view/voice with some consistency	♠ Connections and comparisons (e.g. of theme and style) explored

	1. Knowledge and interpretation of text 2. Exploring language, structure and form 3. Conveying response	Making comparisons (Specification B exam only)
B	♣ Increasingly assured selection and incorporation of relevant detail. Understanding of sub-text ♣ Appreciation of a variety of ways in which effects are achieved ♣ Focused and sustained response	♣ Some sustained discussion of comparisons and relationships between texts
A	♣ Assured selection of key areas of text. Able to speculate/offer tentative judgements in exploring text, taking into account alternative approaches. Evaluation of characters/relationships/situations/attitudes/motives. Able to identify and comment on social/historical and cultural contexts. Awareness of literary tradition shown ♣ Exploration and evaluation of the ways meaning, ideas and feeling are conveyed through language, structure and form ♣ Ideas conveyed coherently. Opinions confidently expressed and insights clearly articulated	♣ Confident exploration of relationships and comparisons between texts, with apt selection of detail for cross-reference.
A*	♣ Text consistently handled with confidence. Overview and ability to move from specific to general ♣ Assured analysis of stylistic features ♣ Cogent and sustained development of literary arguments	♣ Subtle points of comparison probed and explored

Unit 5.1 Responding to extracts

Prose

To Kill a Mockingbird – How does Harper Lee create sympathy in this extract?

(The extract in question is from Chapter 25 of the novel. Tom Robinson has just been killed and Atticus delivers the news to Tom's family. The news of the death spreads around Maycomb and the *Maycomb Tribune* covers the story in a controversial editorial.)

STUDENT RESPONSE TO THE QUESTION

Harper Lee tries to create sympathy in this extract because of the terrible news. She creates sympathy by using the young girl who greets Atticus grinning from ear to ear. Atticus played the father's role by helping her down the steps, but the young girl has no father. 'Atticus went to her, took off his hat and offered her his finger.' This is a very nice gesture to the small girl.

Harper Lee uses Dill to portray how terrible and dramatic it must have been. Dill is very graphic in his description of what happened, 'she just fell down in the dirt … like a giant with a big foot just came along and stepped on her'. Harper Lee uses similes to show the effect of what happened in Dill's words.

Maycomb is portrayed by Harper Lee to be a town that doesn't really care about what happened, as if it is a daily thing, 'Maycomb was interested by the news of Tom's death for perhaps two days'. Prejudice seems to be becoming nastier since the death of Tom, as if Maycomb has not learnt a lesson. How many Black people have to die for them to realise? The society of Maycomb is quite clearly split into two sides, Black society and the white society. We see this even in the newspapers, the Black paper is the 'Coloured news' and the white paper is the 'Maycomb Tribune'.

We see that the 'sin to kill a mockingbird' theme is echoed in the paper, 'he likened Tom's death to the senseless slaughter of songbirds'. This obviously suggests to us that the people of Maycomb do not understand the true meaning of what had been written in the paper and they do not understand what has happened in these last few days.

I Know Why The Caged Bird Sings – How does Maya Angelou portray her mother in this extract?

(The extract in question is from Chapter 9 of the novel.)

The language used in the extract suggests that Maya's mother made a huge impact on Maya and Bailey. In the first sentence Maya says that to describe her mother would be like trying to write about a hurricane. This is Maya's first impression of her mother and she is so overwhelmed by her power she finds she cannot describe her. Maya also says that she feels 'struck dumb' and 'love at first sight'.

Maya uses very beautiful imagery to describe her mother, 'climbing falling colours of a rainbow' and 'my mother's beauty literally assailed me'. She contrasts her momma and her mother, 'momma said it was a sin to wear lipstick'. Momma is very simple, but her mother is the complete opposite and she is almost too complex to start describing.

Maya says that her mother made such an impression on Bailey that he 'fell instantly and forever in love'. This shows how overawed the children are of their mother. The biggest impression her mother made on Maya is how beautiful she is. The whole extract is basically a description of Maya's mother's beauty. When Maya describes her mother she uses natural imagery, 'fresh butter colour'. Also she is impressed by how clean her mother looks, she 'looked see-through clean.' This shows us how Maya was brought up by her momma, cleanliness is very important.

Mother makes her children welcome, 'her smile widened her mouth beyond her cheeks, beyond her ears and seemingly through the walls to the street outside'. This sentence gives the impression of vastness and of their mother's love for them engulfing them. This feeling and her presence in the room are so strong that they had 'forgotten the loneliness and the nights when we had cried together because we were unwanted children'.

Drama

A View From The Bridge – Look closely at the dialogue between Alfieri and Eddie here. How does it create drama for an audience?

(The extract is from Act 1 of the play.)

Eddie, trying to find a reason for Catherine not to marry Rodolfo, makes a fool of himself in this extract. The dark humour in 'He's a blond guy. Like ... platinum. You know what I mean?' creates amusement in the audience at Eddie's prejudice. This is also seen in Alfieri's dialogue when he says, 'Well, that's a tenor'.

Eddie's disbelief at what Alfieri tells him increases along with the tension in the scene. He tries to explain his *thoughts, 'he takes the dress, lays it on the table, he cuts it up; one-two-three, he makes a new dress'.*

Eddie persists, becoming more and more agitated, raising the tension. 'You mean to tell me that there's no law that a guy which ain't right can go to work and marry a girl and_?'

To this outburst, Alfieri replies with the same conviction, 'you have no recourse in the law, Eddie'.

The audience witnesses Eddie's anger and frustration that he cannot do anything legally to prevent the two from marrying. They see that it is possible that Eddie will try other means to achieve this, and as the tension is reaching its climax, it becomes increasingly likely that he will succeed.

The Merchant of Venice – Show how Shakespeare creates dramatic tension for an audience in this extract.

(The extract is from Act IV Scene i of the play.)

STUDENT RESPONSE TO THE QUESTION

Shakespeare uses many different techniques in this extract to create dramatic tension. Firstly, Portia asks 'Is he not able to discharge the money?' the answer being 'yea', shows there is a glimmer of hope that Shylock may take his 'principle' and let Antonio go. Yet Portia states that 'it must not be, there is no power in Venice can alter a decree established'. By giving the reader hope and then destroying this hope, Shakespeare is generating emotion in the audience.

Shylock's rejoicing, 'a Daniel come to judgement', is disheartening for the ones within the audience that support Antonio's plea for mercy. Portia then confirms that 'this bond is forfeit'. By this time there is significant tension mounting within the court and between the characters. But, again Portia gives Shylock the chance to 'be merciful'.

Once Shylock states that 'I stay here on my bond', the tension increases by the sentence, as Portia tells Antonio to 'lay bare your bosom' ready for Shylock's knife. This prolonged arguing over the letter of the bond does not only increase tension but while it is unbearably harrowing it also remorselessly condemns Shylock.

Unit 5.1 Comments on the student responses

Prose – *To Kill a Mockingbird*

In this answer, the student responds to the text fairly sensitively and in some detail, though perhaps with a little uncertainty. The coverage of the text extract is reasonably thorough, for detailed comments are made on different aspects, namely Tom's family, the wider Maycomb community and finally the newspaper. However, there is no initial location of the extract and this sets off a rather haphazard series of comments. The points made are adjacent to the question, rather than focused on it. There is certainly good knowledge of the text, but some limitation in the way that points are explained. Despite the use of quotations, the points made about Maycomb are rather general. (Grade: D/C.)

Prose – *I Know Why The Caged Bird Sings*

This response is unassumingly skilful from the opening line. It is a confident generalization, followed by a worthy attempt to deal with the writer's comparison of the mother to a hurricane. While not explaining with complete authority, the student does sustain the strength of impact through selection of details and the sense of words failing her. Sensible use of contrasts, imagery and, though unnamed, hyperbole move the commentary on effectively, the student consistently making comments that are well-judged. The character and values of Maya's mother are comfortably communicated by the student in this response, with reference to a judicious mixture of content and technique. (Grade: A/A*.)

Drama – *A View From The Bridge*

This is not a long answer, but it is quite astute. The commentary is dominated by vocabulary that aptly represents the tension and conflict (and even humour) in the drama, even though the two characters here are not truly in opposition, for Alfieri is cast in the role of Eddie's troubled ally. The student appears to write as though s/he is instinctively in tune with the dilemma at the heart of the play, with strong engagement in the judgement of reactions – 'disbelief', 'persists', 'outburst', 'conviction'. The contextualizing of the scene is done with an unfussy reference to the encroaching climax of the play. Perhaps the brevity of the response might compromise the outcome a little, but there is no doubt about the essential quality of this answer. (Grade: B/A.)

Drama – *The Merchant of Venice*

This answer misses a golden opportunity to state clearly from the start that the extract is part of a very dramatic courtroom scene in which the stakes are as high as they could be. Failure to do this means that the writing moves forward uncertainly. There is no mention of Bassanio's desperate offer and little sense of Portia's brinkmanship and Shylock's imminent disappointment. To be fair there are several relevant points made by using the text, but the answer lacks a true sense of immediacy and impact. Some summative comments are quite helpful, not least the phrase 'unbearably harrowing', but this really only highlights the student's failure to represent the drama of the moment throughout the rest of the answer. (Grade: D/C.)

Unit 5.2 Discursive essay questions

Prose

To Kill a Mockingbird **– What do you think is the importance of Dill to the novel as a whole?**

Dill is Scout and Jem's long term summer holiday friend. 'Dill was from Meridien, Mississippi' and spent 'the summer with his aunt, Miss Rachel.' Dill is short for 'Charles Baker Harris' an embarrassing name to have and the subject of a lot of teasing.

The fact that Dill has an unusual name and 'is right puny looking' is partly the reason that he boasts appallingly and his speech is riddled with incredible claims that he feels would increase the respect the other children have for him. This is mostly because he does not have one secure home. He is 'passed around relatives' and so does not really fit in anywhere. The fact that he is without a home and therefore without an 'acceptable' background means that he is in fact an outcast. Jem and Scout embrace Dill as their good friend and so demonstrate Atticus's attitude towards people. Atticus's humanity and fair treatment of others is reflected in the way Jem and Scout treat Dill.

Amid the dense storyline, there is a need of some 'light relief' and humour. Dill entertains the readers on numerous occasions within the book. For instance, when Dill tries to explain to Scout – in a superior manner – that 'you could order' a baby from a man 'that rowed across a foggy island where the babies were'.

Dill is also a symbol of the children's fun and games. When they play their games, Dill is ever-present. As they begin to play games less and less as they mature, Dill and Jem become better friends and Scout becomes Dill's wife-to-be! As Dill grows up, we know that time is passing by, and that Jem and Scout are maturing too.

Dill demonstrates his maturity by commenting that Miss Stephanie and Miss Rachel 'should be riding broomsticks'. His saying this shows that he has a mind of his own and thinks things through. An interesting point about Dill is that he is anti-prejudice, as he was very upset by the way 'Mr Gilmer' was 'talking hateful to' Tom

Robinson at the trial. Though the more Scout and Jem 'told Dill about the Radleys, the more he wanted to know.' He wanted to 'try and make Boo come out'. So, Dill is anti-racist yet is the most enthusiastic about tormenting a vulnerable white man.

I Know Why The Caged Bird Sings – **Write about the relationship between Maya and Bailey Junior as they grow up, and how it changes and develops.**

Maya and Bailey Junior's relationship develops and grows throughout the book. However, some things stay the same like the love they feel for each other – even if it is tested at some points.

From a young age Bailey and Maya have had to depend on each other for comfort and for someone to talk to in their time of need, they try do most things together like learning and playing. Maya describes them to 'rattle off the times tables' together and go over what they learnt. We also learn that they grieve and cry together and share the same emotions – 'and nights we had cried together', which suggests their closeness. Twins often feel each other's pain or discomfort because they are so closely matched; in some ways I think Bailey and Maya could be compared to twins as their feelings for each other are so strong. In Stamps they do most things together, 'Bailey and I' is a phrase used a lot in the beginning of the novel which indicates that they're pretty much inseparable.

However, when they meet their parents their feelings for each other change and Maya feels like she's being replaced as Bailey's companion and close friend. Near the beginning of the novel, Maya informs us that Bailey was 'my only brother' and that she had 'no sisters to share with him'. We can also tell that she really admires and adores Bailey and she's so lucky that he 'loves' her even though she's the complete contrast to him and feels that she's 'ugly'. Therefore when their parents enter the picture, Maya surely feels that she's got another sibling to contend with for his affections.

This results in Maya not liking her parents and not really making any efforts to get on well with them. After her father arrives she says that her 'seven-year-old world humpty-dumptied, never to be put back together again', which tells us how uncertain she feels about meeting them. When she meets her mother she feels over-powered by jealousy because she says 'they were more alike than he and I' which indicates that she feels deserted by Bailey because he's giving attention to his mother. This really tested their relationship to the limit because Maya felt betrayed.

The incident with Mr Freeman also affects their relationship greatly. This is the first secret Maya had 'ever kept from Bailey'. This indicates that Maya's beginning to feel isolated and feels like she's growing apart from Bailey. However, she does hope that he would 'read it on my face' by sadly Bailey didn't which reinforces the fact that Maya feels alienated. We also find out that before Mr Freeman attacks Maya, Bailey and her go out but to different places – her to the 'library' and he goes to 'play baseball'. This is a clear contrast to when they were in Stamps when they used to do a lot together and the phrase 'Bailey and I' was repeated many times. This also tells us that Bailey wasn't protecting Maya from Mr Freeman as he was out busy playing with his friends – this shows that they are growing apart.

However, after the family find out about the rape, Bailey tells Maya that there's no danger of him getting hurt and that he'll fight anyone who did this, and their relationship becomes as solid as a rock once more. We also find that when Mr Freeman threatens Maya she stays faithful to Bailey because she doesn't tell a soul. This suggests that their relationship is very strong and withstands everything.

Drama

The Tempest by William Shakespeare – For which character in the play do you have most sympathy? Write about them and their part in the play, and show clearly why they have your sympathy.

The character in the play I feel most sympathy for in the play is Miranda who is Prospero's daughter.

She was also on the ship during the storm which then caused them to arrive on the island as the ship was a wreck.

Miranda is 15 years of age and I feel that she has had rather a sheltered life. As she only knows two other males her father Prospero and Caliban who once tried to rape her. It is not until later on in the play that she meets Ferdinand who she falls madly in love with.

Miranda is a quiet young lady who is mature for her age. Miranda did not know anything about her childhood until her father decided to tell her in Act 1 Scene two where he says

'Hear a little further And then I'll bring thee to the present business.'

Whenever Prospero talks to Miranda she always replies with a sensitive, mature and loyal response. During the play we see how close Prospero is to Miranda.

When Miranda first meets Ferdinand she asks her Father was he a spirit. As she does not understand or has not seen any other men on the island. But when she realises that he is human and not a spirit she falls in love with him.

We see how much Miranda respects her father by the way she says to Ferdinand

'I have broke your heart to say so'

As Miranda has told Ferdinand her name and she is not supposed to tell anyone her name. Miranda does not even know any other women except herself when she looks into her mirror and sees her reflection.

Miranda talks direct to Ferdinand as she did in Act three Scene 1 where she says that she will marry Ferdinand. This part is also similar to Romeo and Juliet where Juliet asks Romeo to marry her.

I think that without Miranda the play would not be able to move on and would be very short as Miranda is one of the main characters with her father. At the end Miranda marries Ferdinand and her father Prospero gives up his magic and breaks his staff.

In some ways you can not say that Miranda is the main character as both Prospero and Miranda work together through the text.

An Inspector Calls by J.B. Priestley – What do you think are the most important factors that contributed to Eva Smith's death?

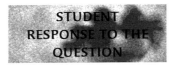

STUDENT RESPONSE TO THE QUESTION

There are several important factors that contributed to Eva Smith's death – the actions and behaviour of Mr and Mrs Birling, the relationship with Gerald and with Eric. It is the accumulation of these various factors which, I believe drove Eva Smith to take her own life.

Mr Birling is a bumptious, conceited and a 'hard-headed business man'. His primary concern is therefore his business, and his wealth. All his speeches in Act One, whilst beginning with the expression of his happiness for his daughter's engagement, ended with discussion of business and 'prosperity'.

The Inspector instigates Birling to admit his involvement with Eva Smith. He had employed her nearly two years before her death. However, he sacked her from her position because she had the audacity to ask for an increase in pay. Mr Birling 'refused, of course'. Eva Smith disrespectfully opposed Mr Birling, 'She'd had a lot to say – far too much – so she had to go'.

Birling's blinkered and dogmatic beliefs and his greed for money contributed to the death of Eva Smith as he used his power – his authority and class and wealth – to force Eva Smith to leave, making her redundant and unable to provide for herself.

Mrs Birling, like her husband, also abused her power, authority and influence to ensure that Eva Smith was not helped by the Brimley Women's Charity Organisation. She admits herself as being 'prejudiced against her case' because Eva called her 'Mrs Birling'. Mrs Birling felt this was a deliberate sign of 'gross impertinence' and insolence. Yet, despite Eva's death, she still felt no remorse or compassion.

Mrs Birling defends her decision before the Inspector, stating 'Yes, it was' her influence, as a prominent member of the community, that finally refused to give Eva Smith any help, insisting that Eva Smith simply did not make the right claims. Mrs Birling intimates that she was a liar and disrespectful and thus justifies her decision to have the claim refused.

Sheila, however, though she played a significant part in contributing to her death cannot be condemned as much as her parents. Sheila confesses she got Eva Smith sacked from Milward's because she was jealous of her beauty and used her influence to ensure she was made redundant, 'I told him that if they didn't get rid of that girl, I'd never go near the place again ... I'd persuade mother to close our account with them.'

Gerald Croft claims that he didn't 'Install her (Eva Smith) there so that I could make love to her' but in order to help her. He rescued her from the advances of a local drunk, Joe Meggarty, and gave her food, shelter and stability. However, unintentionally, he ended the affair badly and abruptly and this inevitably made Eva Smith feel awfully used and manipulated.

To make matters worse, Eric became involved with her also and made her pregnant, but she ended the relationship although he offered her money. She then turned to Mrs Birling for help.

It is quite evident that although each of the characters were linked to Eva Smith, like rings on a chain, no one knew about the other. Each character betrayed Eva Smith morally – they each manipulated Eva's lack of authority and low social class. Mr and Mrs Birling used social politics to justify their actions. These blinkered views of class and lack of responsibility were apparent in each relationship. This is the most important factor which contributed to Eva Smith's death – the lack of responsibility for one's own actions – but also the lack of community. The lack of compassion and human decency to help someone in trouble, asking for nothing in return.

Unit 5.2 Comments on the student responses

Prose – *To Kill a Mockingbird* – Dill

This response does not focus immediately on the question. Instead, there is a sense of the student wishing to off-load all the available information about Dill. By the end of the second paragraph, however, the connections have been made, if not explicitly, at least by strong implication. In the course of the answer, the student refers to the values, the tone, the symbolism and the irony of Dill's role in the novel, so this is an answer with reasonably strong awareness of the deeper meaning of the novel. Yet, some comments are not fully explained and the essay as a whole is not convincingly cohesive. (Grade: C/B.)

Prose – *I Know Why The Caged Bird Sings* – Maya and Bailey Junior

The student here provides a genuinely discursive response to a task that is not actually set in question form, but which requires focus on the changing and developing relationship of Maya and Bailey Junior. There is a good balance to the essay, with a clear range of incidents and 'chapters' involved. The selecting and highlighting is very effective and the points coherent, well explained and linked. (Grade: B/A.)

Drama – *The Tempest* – Miranda

This is a straightforward response that offers general information about Miranda, the chosen character, in the story, rather than explores the key scenes of the play in which she appears. The question is dealt with in an unfocused way – there is little attempt to judge why one should feel great sympathy for Miranda and there is some contradiction in the way she is described as mature, but has little experience of life. The quotations, too, are not well chosen and the comments on them are not particularly successful. It is clear that the student has reasonable recall of the play, and it is possible to see how the essay could have been stronger with just a little more organization and planning. (Grade: E/D.)

Drama – *An Inspector Calls* – Eva Smith's death

This is an extremely purposeful answer to the question. The clear thinking and organized analysis is excellent, as is the judgement of expression with which the words and actions of the characters is explained. The student's vocabulary is strong enough to expose each character individually and the choice of quotations is apt for the characters to expose themselves. The response is of good length and it never falters in its purpose. The conclusion confirms the student's understanding of the moral strength of the play. (Grade: A/A*.)

Unit 5.3 Empathy questions

Prose

To Kill a Mockingbird – Imagine you are Atticus. Write down your thoughts after the trial of Tom Robinson.

STUDENT RESPONSE TO THE QUESTION

It was the last few days of the trial and I felt great anticipation, but at the same time I felt like I was fighting an already lost battle. When the trial started the first person I questioned was Mr Tate the local sheriff. He seemed quite nervous when I spoke to him as if he was hiding something, but I do not know what. I asked him what eye did Mayella have bruising on, he was not sure, then he realised that it must have been the left. I realised at that moment that it would have been difficult for Tom to hit her when one of his arms was crippled.

I couldn't understand how ignorant and prejudiced Bob Ewell is, people like him are the culprits that wreck the Ewell's already poor reputation. In my mind, I could tell it was him that attacked his daughter, but I had no way of proving this. Also the court was against me.

I started asking Mr Ewell questions, questions he was struggling to answer. I asked him why he didn't call a doctor, he replied he didn't think to and it would have cost him five dollars! I tried my last few questions to Bob, I asked if he was left handed or not. I already knew the answer that he was left handed, which I had tried to portray to the judges that most of Mayella's injuries were on the right side of her face, which suggests that a right handed man did this. One thing I taught Jem and Scout is to never ask a witness or criminal a question you do not know the answer to.

My final impressions of Bob is that he was cocky, coarse and had no feelings for Mayella. I know he did it but I must find a way to prove it.

Of Mice And Men by John Steinbeck – Imagine you are Slim. What are your thoughts as you look back on the events at the ranch involving George and Lennie?

'I remember the whole business now. Of course, George still works here on the ranch. After Lennie died, he eventually decided to try to hold down a job. But the spark's gone from him now — he and Lennie were more than just travelling companions. They were closer than I've ever seen two guys.

The incident affected many people on the ranch pretty badly — probably George worst of all. After he shot Lennie, I took him for a drink and tried to console him. But George just threw down whiskey after whiskey and didn't say much, from time to time he mumbled the odd sentence about a childhood memory. But hell, I don't think I've ever seen a guy so down and depressed. I know it was the right thing to do — Curley would have had him strung up or shot him in the guts. But that wouldn't have been no good. Candy was hit very badly — he got the can two weeks later and was very upset, not only because he'd lost a friend in Lennie, but because of something else which he told me about in private soon after. It seems that George, Lennie and Candy were one month away from packing in their jobs and buying their own place.

The boss wasn't particularly happy at losing Lennie either — he said he thought that Lennie was the best damn worker we've ever had on this ranch. He was certainly the strongest. The boss apparently didn't trust the pair of them when they first turned up, but one day when he saw Lennie shifting barley bags into a cart, and lifting them as if they were feathers, damn nearly killing the two men struggling behind him, he was won over. I was certainly pleased to have such a good worker on my team — it made life a whole lot easier and made a change from the pair of punks that he had replaced.

I was shocked when I saw the reaction of Carlson and the others after Lennie had died — they couldn't understand why George was so depressed. The man had just shot his best friend — surely that's reason enough to be slightly unhappy. I think I understood what George was going through, but there was really very little I could do other than listen to him.

Of course, Curley's wife was buried the next day. I always felt sorry for her — she was always so lost, lonely and out of place, being the only woman on the ranch. I never thought Curley looked after her — and because of that and her flirting all the time, I guess she was a death trap waiting to happen. Curley, that heartless bastard, didn't even shed a tear at the funeral. Even when he had just seen his own wife killed, and I advised him to stay with her, he seemed more concerned with settling an old score with Lennie. Sure enough he's already been seen strutting around the ranch with a new woman — I only hope she doesn't go the same way.

Lennie was only with us for a short time, but even that seemed to pass very quickly, I could see from the beginning that although he was dumb as hell, he was a nice guy deep down, and would never deliberately hurt anyone.

Drama

A View From The Bridge – Imagine you are a policeman in the neighbourhood. After Eddie's death you interview the people involved. Write up two of these interviews. Remember to think about how your chosen characters would speak and behave.

Interview 1 – With Beatrice

Police: How did Eddie interact with Marco?

Beatrice: Eddie had no problem with Marco the problem lay with Rodolfo.

P   How so?

B   From the day they arrived, Eddie was convinced that Rodolfo was gay. His suspicions were given further evidence when he found out that Rodolfo could sing and make dresses.

P   How did this lead to the fight with Marco?

B   For several years, we have been looking after Catherine. When Rodolfo arrived, they fell in love. However, Eddie had also become attracted to Catherine and he was so jealous that he went to extreme measures. When the idea that Rodolfo was just after his papers, he went to see Alfieri, who admits that his only alternative is the immigration.

P   And he told, on both of them?

B   Yes, and Marco was feeding his starving children, and so claimed that he killed his wife and children.

P   Thank you, Beatrice, you've been very helpful.

Interview 2 – With Rodolfo

Police: I believe that you are, all be it, indirectly, the cause of this tradegy.

Rodolfo: How can you say that?

P   You dated Catherine, did you not?

R   Yes, but I don't see the connection.

P   Did you ask for Eddie's permission?

R   I didn't think that would be necessary.

P   Why not?

R   He is not her father.

P   Yes, but he's looked after her for many years, don't you feel that the honourable thing to do was to ask?

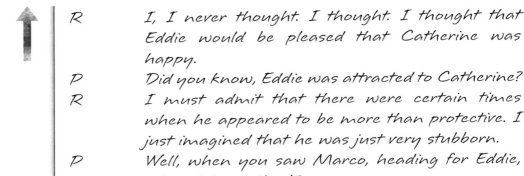

R	*I, I never thought. I thought. I thought that Eddie would be pleased that Catherine was happy.*
P	*Did you know, Eddie was attracted to Catherine?*
R	*I must admit that there were certain times when he appeared to be more than protective. I just imagined that he was just very stubborn.*
P	*Well, when you saw Marco, heading for Eddie, what did you think?*
R	*I was amazed. I didn't think Eddie would be so cruel as to send us back, and I didn't think Marco would be so foolish.*
P	*Thank you for the help. We'll be back in touch.*
R	*Any time.*

The Merchant of Venice – Imagine you are Antonio. Write down your thoughts after the trial has ended.

STUDENT RESPONSE TO THE QUESTION

How I wish this whole messy business had never occurred! And yet perhaps that is not true. After all, my good friend Bassanio has found a true and loving wife and repaid his debts, a grasping and malicious villain has been brought to justice and to the light of Christianity and my luck has turned and I still live to see the joy of my friends.

Looking back on the past few months of my life I can see how foolish and over-confident I have been. I was too hasty, too willing to put my trust in my ships. I believed that my ventures were 'not in one bottom trusted' and that I could clear my bond with Shylock well before the arranged date. When that cunning dog presented the terms of the bond to me as if it were 'a merry sport', I could see no catch, no stumbling block and, ignoring Bassanio's warning, I recklessly agreed to the bond, thinking there was 'much kindness in the Jew'.

I would suffer anything for Bassanio, my most dear of friends and although he still owed me a sum of money, no such thought entered my head when he asked me for the sum of three thousand ducats. I had faith in him and hurt when he seemed to feel he had to excuse himself to me, he did me more wrong.

In making question of my uttermost, than if he had wasted everything I own. I felt shamed when I was forced to do business with such a fellow as the Jew, I have always furnished my friends with money as an act of kindness, not to gain profit as is all the greedy usurer is concerned with. I have always known the man to have a deep and painful hatred for all Christians but could not expect to see in any human being the revengeful, malicous spirit which prompted him to attempt my life. He was man driven to a beast by the hatred inside him. I fell deeper and deeper into a state of depression and fear as I heard news of my ships, wrecked at sea, one 'ship of rich lading' lay buried on the Goodwins 'a very dangerous flat' and I knew in my heart that it was mine own.

I allowed myself no hope and refused to think of my friend Bassanio lest in my despair I lost the strong faith I had in him. I prayed only that his fortune had been good and some happiness had come of the terrible bond. As the time grew closer and my ships had not returned, Shylock began to bait me, jeering and repeating 'I'll have my bond'. I knew then that such was the hatred inside him that his soul was turned to the devil and that no pleading could make him show mercy. I resigned myself to the end and determined to show a calm dignity which would take the pleasure from the man's revenge. I could only feel regret that such an incident should be allowed to happen and pity for the young, fresh-faced judge who could only do his job. His words or indeed her words, as I later discovered, 'Tarry a little, there is something else' struck a ray of hope into my heart and the turmoil within me made it difficult to react to the people around me as the wise and clever Portia saved my life. As indeed she did.

Unit 5.3 Comments on the student responses

Prose – *To Kill A Mockingbird* – Atticus

This is a fairly competent account of some main parts of Tom Robinson's trial as experienced by Atticus Finch. It is coherent, and though not especially well developed, the points made are more than fleeting and manage to convey a sound view. This amounts to good knowledge of (relatively) minor characters. In addition, there is an isolated insight into Atticus as a parent. Where the response is a little disappointing is in the failure to establish a clear voice for Atticus, one that would leave no doubt as to his convictions and frustrations. (Grade: C/B.)

Prose – *Of Mice And Men* – Slim

In this response, an authentic-sounding Slim is established from the start and his voice is sustained throughout with great effect. His thoughts and feelings show clear insight into characters and relationships and Slim's views of other characters. The student's knowledge of the text shines through consistently, with excellent selection of detail reinforcing the portrayal of the character. Slim is sensitive but not sentimental in this portrayal. The invented details, e.g. the funeral, are kept in due proportion and are included to shed appropriate insights into characters. (Grade: A/A*.)

Drama – *A View From The Bridge* – Beatrice/Rodolfo

The student here is never quite comfortable with the script format, though the approach is quite valid, indeed appropriate, for this task. The policeman/interviewer could provide impetus in a response by intervening purposefully in Beatrice and Rodolpho's statements, but in this example it appears that the pace is slowed down by fairly neutral questioning. Simply, there is too much of the policeman and not enough of Beatrice and Rodolfo. Nevertheless, there is good awareness of the text and its issues, and some selection of detail. There is a sense of the differing standpoints of the characters, but no real difference in their voices. (Grade: D/C.)

Drama – *The Merchant of Venice* – Antonio

This is an impressive response that succeeds easily in developing Antonio's attitude and character through the integration of textual detail. The way quotations are incorporated into the text is particularly pleasing. Antonio is portrayed as a complex character, essentially a melancholic individual, and this is conveyed through his stoical unselfishness. The coverage of the text is considerable. Although there may be interpretations of Antonio's character that could be more revelatory and less enigmatic, this particular representation sustains the mystery of the original. (Grade: A/A*.)

Unit 5.4 Poetry appreciation

NOTE All the student responses in this section are to the question: **Write about the poem and its effect on you.**

'Laugharne Castle' by John Idris Jones

STUDENT RESPONSE TO THE QUESTION

This poem describes how a castle is still standing on a cliff after centuries of time and how the poet feels respect and admiration for it. The castle is at first described as a ruin; it sounds like only the two end walls have survived and the middle part of the castle has collapsed, 'like curtains left after a play'. The poet's initial opinion of the castle is not good; it sounds like an unsightly eyesore that should be ignored or demolished, 'brown as mud, holed, ivied, roofless'. The phrase 'a straggled jetsam' makes it sound like it has washed up on the shore from a shipwreck.

I feel the poet wants us to recognise the beauty of this ancient monument. He describes the 'mud glistens' and the castle still remains against the 'ooze of tides'. I think he may feel disappointed that his castle like many others, is neglected. However he realises the old walls, 'without improvement' tell their own history.

The tone of this poem, I feel, may be bitter. The castle is deserted and no-one seems to care, it is hidden 'against the cliff'. I also feel the tone may be calm: the 'sea swings', changing the sand. The alliteration emphasises the imagery created, the atmosphere appears relaxed.

The poem is presented in four stanzas each read as one sentence, which quickens the pace of reading.

I feel the end of this poem is suggesting that an old 'eye and a hand,' elderly person admires watching the castle. This person may remember the stories, 'representing' them. Maybe the poet is suggesting that not all is forgotten.

I feel this poem made the castle come to life. It changes with time and ages, the 'shoulders of mud are old but strong'. Descriptive detail creates a calm image of the castle, retiring at its home along the coast.

'Cameraman' by Sheenagh Pugh

'Cameraman' by Sheenagh Pugh is a mantra for cameramen. They have to battle with their emotions when filming the horrific scenes of countries affected by disasters such as war. There are many themes throughout this poem, but the most pervading idea is of duty: the camera mans duty to report the events he is witnessing impartially and honestly. This is shown in the first stanza:

'You must turn away from nothing.'

Sheenagh Pugh's choice of language in this stanza reinforces this commandment and words such as 'all' and 'must' are repeated throughout, leading the reader to feel that a cameraman is compelled by the discipline to follow this code. She uses direct speech to involve the reader directly in the poem, but it is the cameraman that is being addressed.

The second most prevalent theme is compassion. At first the forbidding tone of the second stanza misled me to believe that a cameraman must not be compassionate:

'You must not turn your hand
To feed the dying children...'

There are some really troubling images in the poem like the above and the cameraman sees them but has to ignore them.

However, after reading the final stanza I realised that although they must not show compassion personally, by using their camera they can stir thousands of others to show and use their compassion. Pugh explains this in the second stanza.

'You are the itch.'

This poem is set world wide, as cameramen film wherever the story is unfurling. This is because the poem is written as a command to cameramen and subtly praises them.

'You can make them see clear,
if only you watch,'

The camera is your eyes, it is as if it must see the suffering not you. This makes you feel sympathy for the cameraman for having to see all this suffering, even though his senses are dulled. The cameraman is a messenger, he just shows what he saw so you can make others feel and do something.

'Home' by Rupert Brooke

'Home' by Rupert Brookes has a definite theme of the paranormal. In this poem Brookes tells a story that allows the reader to interpret according to his or her beliefs. The man in this poem is describing how his loneliness has affected him. He wants to be with a woman so badly his mind plays tricks on him and he imagines a woman sitting by his fireplace when really there is no one there. This ultimately leaves him feeling even lonelier.

The house at first sounds welcoming and cosy as the man returns 'late and tired'. Even though the room is gloomy, it is still 'comfortable' which makes it sound like a pleasant place to be. The man's attention initially focuses on the 'long chair' which implies that he intends to stretch out and relax after his hard day.

The man's surprise is evident when he notices a woman sitting in his chair by the firelight. He notices every detail of her profile, 'the line of neck and cheek and chin'. Although he is surprised to see her and does not recognise her ('the form of one I did not know'), it takes him a moment before he approaches her. He is almost mesmerised with the sight of her in his 'little room'.

He obviously feels a mixture of emotions upon seeing her; 'I stood a moment fierce and still'. He is trying to overcome his emotions. He is surprised and even angered that someone has entered his room and obviously made themselves at home. But at the same time, he is does not want to disturb her or he is too shocked to move. Again there is the sense that he is mesmerised by what he can see, 'watching her neck and hair'. But when he finally does move towards her, she vanishes, 'there was no one there'. This makes the reader question what has happened. Maybe the man is crazy and hallucinating? Maybe it was just a trick of the firelight because the room is 'gloomy'? Maybe the woman was a ghost? This makes you really want to keep on reading until the end of the poem to find out how the man will react to this.

The man confesses 'it was just a trick of the firelight that made me see her there'. This makes you feel sorry for the man. He seemed to be anticipating seeing someone in his room and this caused his mind to play tricks on him. However, seeing this apparition had a very negative effect on him. It reinforces his sense of loneliness and makes him even more aware of his desperate situation. He was disturbed all night by thoughts of this woman and thoughts of his loneliness, 'that night, how could I sleep?' The atmosphere in the room has changed since he saw the woman sitting in his chair; the gloom is no longer 'comfortable' it is now 'lonely'. Everything about the room that was welcoming and comforting has been changed and is now cold and lonely. Instead of watching the firelight, he spent the night watching the 'moonlight creep from wall to basin'. This is a stark contrast to the way the room was before. Everything now seems to reinforce the idea that he is feeling isolated and lonely.

'Song' by W.H. Auden

I feel, this poem basically conveys how love can become more important than anything in many peoples lives. The author does not just portray how love affects an individual. Instead, he targets their occupation, to label them with a name. I believe a moment in time is consistent throughout this poem as the author first begins the poem by informing us of how 'Chimney sweepers' are affected by love and concluding with how 'Inspectors' are affected by love. W. H. Auden does this to convey that love can affect anyone.

Throughout this poem no strict setting is important. This again adds to the tone of the poem by making who they are, what they are or where they are of no importance because they can still be affected by love. I receive the impression that W. H. Auden writes in a tone that conveys neither a negative nor positive attitude to love. However, he shows throughout the poem what is affected by love. He begins to reveal what he believes affects a person in love by talking of appearance, 'wash their faces and forget to wash the neck,' this portrays that the way they look is important as they want to make a good impression. This becomes more important than the actual job, 'wash the neck'. The prosperous baker is willing to risk his positive position for love, again we are informed of what W. H. Auden believes to be an effect of love, risking every thing. Again I feel W H. Auden's attitude to love is portrayed showing how various characters in this poem give up everything to make love their first priority. This is conveyed by 'Wait till return', this is a statement of an undertaker losing time and respect for others over love.

This poem has one narrative voice and that is the author W. H. Auden. I believe this has a strong effect on the poem because it provides the author with a chance to express his opinions. I also believe that this poem, having one narrative voice, shows that he has noticed other peoples actions and has analysed them to conclude on what effects love can have a people, the basic tone of the poem.

Due to the structure the poem only in the last line of the second stanza does it become apparent the all characters are dropping what they are doing to 'Keep their date with love'. The structure of the poem is written as a 'song'. However, this is subtly conveyed by using rhyming language in each stanza, to set a pace. W. H. Auden uses language such as 'sweepers and keepers' in stanza one to portray the other actors have something in common, they are all in love.

This poem creates the image of the world coming to a stand still, as we are informed of people walking away from everything important. I also believe the way in which W. H. Auden describes the effect the engine-drivers have by saying 'Bring expresses in the tunnel to a stop', this again portrays a slowing down in time or a complete stand still.

'The Film' by John Cotton

The poem 'The film' is about a person cleaning out a relatives house after they have died. They find a camera with a film still in it which has pictures of the deceased's family on it.

The poet uses very effective words to describe their last visit together when the person was still well. John Cotton makes you feel as if he is trying to tell you not to waste your last moments and to live for everyday. The poet uses words like intimate to describe the way he felt when he was there with the person.

The mood makes you want to really think about what is going on. It is a very sad poem in some ways because the person he is talking about is now gone forever, but in other ways it is also happy remembering the happy times that the person and their family shared together.

The poet has written the poem very cleverly, because the first verse concentrates on the loss that they are feeling but the second verse is remembering the happiness that was felt.

I think this poem was very effective and striking. It really made me feel about what John Cotton was trying to get across. I think the poet wrote this to write what he felt when maybe, one of his relatives died and he wanted us to understand what it feels like to lose somebody like he did. I liked this poem because it made me think about his loss.

'Background Material' by Tony Harrison

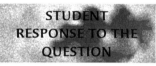

The poem obviously concerns the writer's family and his thoughts about them. The title 'Background Material' is suggested by the situation as he looks at the photos but also refers to his family background and to his work as a writer.

The photos themselves are 'neither one a couple and both bad' which gives the impression of distance or lack of communication in the family. Perhaps his dad has left his mother, or died –

'My father and his background are both gone,'
whereas his mother is still present in his life –
'but hers ... still shows'
This shows that some of his mother lives on in him, in his cottage. However, even here change is emphasised –
'though only the greenness of it's stayed the same.'

The mood of the poem is nostalgic and there is an element of pathos running all through it as though the writer is sad and there is some unknown (to the reader) tragedy that has happened.

The poem is split into five unequal stanzas possibly showing the different stages of the poet's recollections. In fact there are really three sections to the poem: setting the scene as he sits at his writing desk; looking at the background to the pictures and thinking about how times have changed; reflecting on his own relationship with his father and mother. The end of the poem brings us back to his present situation and somehow emphasises a sense of isolation.

The pace of the poem changes as he recollects memories of his family. The first stanza seems to slow as he reminisces. Then, as he looks closely at the photographs, the last seven lines are in a single sentence, but this is split up as if he is thinking deeply and carefully. You feel that he is searching his own feelings as he examines the photos. I think that the poet wishes to remember his parents as a couple, but can't as he has no photographs of them together. He is the only link between them.

The language of the poem is mainly simple and everyday (e.g. 'mam', 'pub') but it still creates quite an enigmatic quality. The poet uses repetition quite effectively in the second stanza ('gone … gone', 'same … same) and in the last section imagery of light ('colour', 'gleam', 'light') perhaps inferring that his memories are filled with light and joy. However, my main impression is of sadness, and this is re-emphasised by the image of a shadow at the end of the poem.

Unit 5.4 Comments on the student responses

'Laugharne Castle'

This is a pleasing response, sensible and methodical in its use of detail and accompanying comments. It is thoughtful, even in the comments made on imagery and form. The writing is comfortably in tune with the mood and atmosphere of the poem. There is opportunity perhaps to develop the poem's sense of history and Welshness, but the length of the response is more than adequate as it stands. (Grade: B/A.)

'Cameraman'

This answer is strong and confident. There is a clear attempt from the start to establish voice and situation and the bluntness of the poem is reflected well in the response. The details of language may not have been explored to the full, but the use of the text is clearly satisfactory and the overview of the poem is well established. (Grade: B/A.)

'Home'

This is an answer of high quality which is also sustained well beyond reasonable expectation in the time available. It is not a response that follows the bullet points rigidly, so it might be seen not to be dealing with certain features explicitly, while in fact the structure of the response follows closely the development of the poem. To assess this piece on a deficit model, i.e. judging it by what is missing, would be extremely harsh. (Grade: A/A*.)

'Song'

This is a commendable effort on a poem that is not easy to write about, because it has no 'place' and no 'character' as a focus. The student does well to make philosophical points of interest out of the snapshots that the poem offers. Some overall coherence is present too, as well as a genuine determination to deal with form and structure. The effect is undermined by some loose expression (there is much redundancy) and organization, but the willingness to probe the poem is pleasing. (Grade: C/B.)

'The Film'

This response shows a general grasp of the meaning of the poem. There is an awareness of the happiness and the sadness of the tone, and the student begins to look at the structure of the poem. However, overall there is a lack of detailed appreciation. Comments tend to be clear but straightforward, remaining at a simple level. (Grade: E/D.)

'Background Material'

This answer combines overview with attention to detail and sensible speculation. Some points could be developed further, but there is a good attempt to tackle structure. Despite the lack of explanation, this is an assured response. (Grade: A/A*.)

Unit 5.5 Anthology comparison tasks

Prose

For this answer you will need to write about how places affect characters in two stories.

First, look at *Bella Makes Life*. How does life in America change Bella?

Now look at *The Lesson*. How is Sylvia affected by her surroundings in this story?

Thinking of the two stories, which character's reaction to place do you find more interesting, and why?

NOTE Both of these stories remain in the WJEC Anthology for 2005–07.

STUDENT RESPONSE TO THE QUESTION

Bella has greatly changed during her stay in America. This the reader sees through many things. We see through Jojo's reaction to her, and comments that she has changed and we also see through the letters which are a stylistic feature of the story.

We see straight away on the first line that Bella is different in Jojo's eyes:
'He was embarrassed' (line 1).

This immediately shows that something is different and unexpected about Bella as he wouldn't normally be embarrassed meeting his wife.

The first thing that has changed about Bella is her clothes:
'What was this woman doing dressed like this? (line 7)

We see that this is a change through Jojo's reactions:
'See you Jesus!' (line 10).

The letters chart Bella's transition in America. They start loving and intimate:
'Dear Jojo' and 'I'm saving all my love for you' (line 25) and then we see her becoming more wrapped up in her life in America:
'I figure I might as well enjoy myself' (line 37) and more formal:
'Dear Joseph' (line 29)

Bella has also changed by becoming much more ambitious:
'You have to make it'

She seems to have adopted the American dream of making it big and is no longer content with the simple Jamaican life:
'Box feeding outta hog mouth' (line 137)

Bella views her life with Jojo now as poor and deprived.

Bella's change in attitude ruins her relationship with Jojo:
'he missed the old Bella' (line 87) and causes her to go back to America, which now suits her more than Jamaica does.

Bella's change is summed up very well by the necklace she wears:
'Material Girl' (line 14)

showing possessions are now more important to her than love.

Sylvia is greatly affected by her change in surroundings in 'The Lesson'. She is extremely confident in her home area:
'me and Sugar were the only ones just right' (line 2)

and she acts how she wants to act and disrespects everyone:

>'we laughed at her' (line 4)
>
>'being surly' (line 32).

This however greatly changes when she goes to a rich area. Here she feels out of place and although she tries to be herself, and give guarded, clever responses to what Miss Moore is trying to teach them she can't hide her surprise at what it's like.

>' "Unbelievable" I hear myself say' (line 123).

She finds herself in awe of her surroundings and she doesn't like it.

>'Watcha bring us here for?' (line 182)

She senses that her and her peers do not belong in a place like this.

>'like a glued-together jigsaw done all wrong' (165)

This simile sums up how they are not part of this society and don't fit in. Because of this Sylvia doesn't know how to act:

>'But we don't laugh and go into our fat lady routine' (179)

This reaction to her surroundings is very surprising as at the beginning of the story it seems that nothing can please her.

I find Sylvia's reaction to her new surroundings more interesting because Bella has been in America for a year so it is not that surprising that she has changed whereas with Sylvia it is much more immediate and with it comes a new realisation of inequality and relating issues that Sylvia has never considered before:

>'this is not much of a democracy if you ask me.'

We also see how Sylvia does not want to face this reality:

>'I am disgusted at Sugar's treachery' (line 223)

This provokes much of a moral question and so I find it more interesting than Bella's response to America.

Poetry

In 'Away and See'*, 'Saying Something'* and 'Valentine', Carol Ann Duffy explores different aspects of love and relationships.

Compare two of these poems making sure you cover the following:
- ♣ What the poet has to say about love in each poem
- ♣ The poet's use of language
- ♣ The way the poems are organized and structured.

*NOTE 'Valentine' remains in the WJEC Anthology for 2005–07, but 'Away and See' and 'Saying Something' are no longer in the Anthology after 2004.

STUDENT RESPONSE TO THE QUESTION

'Saying Something' and 'Valentine' are both poems by Carol Ann Duffy that explore the theme of love. 'Saying Something' is about a long term relationship in which the couple are very content and comfortable. Negative aspects are also explored at the end of the poem. 'Valentine' is about the unorthodox gift of an onion for St. Valentine's Day. Simple words are used to portray a very simplistic interpretation of love.

A similarity between the two poems is that they both portray the goodness of being in love and show the positive aspects. In 'Saying Something' the poet describes the way in which her and her partner are so close and united that they barely need to talk. This portrays the image that they understand each other so well. A metaphor is used to convey this image.

'My heart assumes it.'

Similarly, 'Valentine' shows that love can be a wonderful feeling. Eg The image of the onion is symbolic of love and in the first stanza it is compared to the moon, a traditional symbol of goodness. This shows the poet's positive outlook towards love.

'It promises light'

Both the poems suggest that in a relationship there is no need for constant extravagant gestures and that love can be a simple yet beautiful thing. In 'Saying Something' the poet feels love for her partner so much that even the simplest of everyday objects remind her of him and they are endearing to her. This shows that if you are truly in love even a simple, routine life can be a very happy and rewarding life.

'Things assume your shape;
discarded clothes, a damp shroud.'

In comparison, 'Valentine' also shows that real love can be simple. This is achieved when the poet rejects cliches of love and opts for an onion as a gift. This suggests that stereotypical images of love have no true meaning or depth. The poet believes love should be simple and honest not superficial.

'Not a cute card or a kissogram.'

Another similarity is that both poems show the potential threat of love. In 'Saying Something', the poet considers life without her partner should anything go wrong. This highlights her underlying fear that the relationship may end. The poet feels she would be alone and unhappy without him.

'I dreamed I was not with you.
Wondering in a city ... I stared
At strangers.'

Similarly, 'Valentine' portrays the negative aspects of love. The image that commitment can be destructive and that when relationships end it can be very painful is depicted. This shows the realistic outlook of the poet. Again the image of an onion making you cry is used to show the potential path of love.

'It will blind you with tears like a lover.'

In conclusion, both the poems appear very positive towards love. 'Valentine' appears, however, to be slightly more realistic because a sense of maturity and realism is conveyed throughout the poem. 'Saying Something' appears to be slightly more traditional because the woman appears in awe of her partner and doesn't feel she could ever live without him.

Unit 5.5 Comments on the student responses

Prose – Comparison of *Bella Makes Life* and *The Lesson*

The layout of this piece is not pleasing to the eye and makes the writing appear rather fragmentary, which in fact it is not. The student actually uses short quotations very effectively, integrating them into the flow of the essay, despite appearances. (The line references are unnecessary.) It quickly becomes apparent that this is a formidable response, which deals with both texts thoroughly and with great precision. The section of direct comparison at the end is authoritative and balanced; focused work on each of the stories individually also contributes to the comparative effect. Although the piece has the air of a commentary rather than an essay, the weight of evidence of quality is exceptional. (Grade: A/A*.)

Poetry – Comparison of two poems by Carol Ann Duffy

This essay makes the skill of comparison appear rather easy! The intention is clear from the start to deal with both poems equally and, by the end of the first paragraph, a secure, summarizing comment has been made on each. The links that are made subsequently (often at the start of each paragraph) confirm the sense of an impressively organized piece. It is difficult to maintain successfully an approach to comparison based on consistent cross-referencing, but this student does it very well indeed. Of course, without the quality of comments on the two poems all would not be so impressive, but the student has a good eye for detail and repeatedly makes well-judged, mature comments. (Grade: A/A*.)